SEAFOOD RECIPE COOKBOOK

Enjoy All Types of Delicious Seafood With Easy Seafood Recipes

(A Seafood Cookbook for Effortless Meals)

Victor Wyse

Published by Alex Howard

© **Victor Wyse**

All Rights Reserved

Seafood Recipe Cookbook: Enjoy All Types of Delicious Seafood With Easy Seafood Recipes (A Seafood Cookbook for Effortless Meals)

ISBN 978-1-990169-85-4

All rights reserved. No part of this guide may be reproduced in any form without permission in writing from the publisher except in the case of brief quotations embodied in critical articles or reviews.

Legal & Disclaimer

The information contained in this book is not designed to replace or take the place of any form of medicine or professional medical advice. The information in this book has been provided for educational and entertainment purposes only.

The information contained in this book has been compiled from sources deemed reliable, and it is accurate to the best of the Author's knowledge; however, the Author cannot guarantee its accuracy and validity and cannot be held liable for any errors or omissions. Changes are periodically made to this book. You must consult your doctor or get professional medical advice before using any of the suggested remedies, techniques, or information in this book.

Table of contents

Part 1 1
Antoine's Oysters Rockefeller 2
Artichoke Bottoms with Bay Scallops 3
Art's Mock Crabmeat Casserole 4
Avocado Crabmeat Salad 5
Bacon And Smoked Oysters 6
Bailey's Bouillabaisse (Fish Stew) 7
Baked Clams With Black Bean Sauce 8
Baked Crab Quesadillas 9
Baked Salmon Steaks 11
Barbecue Crab Sandwich 12
Barbecued Catfish 13
Barbecued Salmon With Basil 14
Basic Best Salmon Loaf 15
Basque Style Steamed Clams 16
Brigitte's Shrimp Or Tuna Mousse 17
Brigitte's Tuna Burgers 18
Broiled Bay Scallops 19
Broiled Fish With Devilled Cheese 20
Broiled Monkfish In Gingered Soy Sauce 21
Broiled Seafood Canapés 22
Broken Fish Trap Soup 23
Butterfish With Lemongrass 24
Cajun Fish Fillets 25
California-Style Salmon 26

Camp Tuna & Rice	27
Catfish Chilli	28
Catfish Mexican Style	29
Cheer Up A Crab	30
Cheesy Broiled Flounder	31
Cheesy Salmon Supper	32
Chile Tuna Sea Shells	33
Chinese Oyster Stew	34
Coconut Fish Roe Samba	35
Codfish Vegetable Casserole	36
Confetti Crab Salad	37
Crab And Corn Cakes	38
Crab Broccoli Casserole	39
Crabs With Ginger & Green Onions	40
Crawfish Chilli	41
Cream Of Crab Soup	42
Creamed Lobster & Clams	43
Creole Fish Soup	44
Devilled Crab Croquettes	45
Firecracker Grilled Alaskan Salmon	46
Fried Fish In Spicy Sauce	47
Guianese Curried Fish	48
Gorton's New England Clam Chowder	49
Grilled Spiced Fish	50
Henderson Boiled Crawfish	51
Herbs & Trout	52
Hickory Smoked Salmon	53

High Country Fried Trout	54
Oriental Steamed Fish	55
Oysters Annapolis	56
Pacific Clam & Corn Chowder	57
Penne Pasta With Tuna	58
Pepper's Tuna Casserole	59
Quick Fish Chowder	61
Rainbow Trout Provencal	62
Rotini & Crab	63
Sesame Salmon Steaks	64
Seven Minute Boiled Crawfish	65
Shark Steaks	66
Shrimp Brochette	67
Simple Scallops Supreme	68
So Easy Fish	69
Swordfish Kebabs	70
The Perfect Tuna Casserole	71
Tomato-Fish Cossack Stew	72
Trout Appétit With Remoulade Sauce	73
Tuna Apple Salad	74
Tuna In A Shell	75
Vegetable Fish Fillets	76
Whitefish Baked With Fiddlehead Ferns	78
Chunky Seafood Chowder	79
Seafood Stuffed Mushrooms	79
Special Spicy Seafood Sauce	79
Kahala's Macaroni Seafood Salad	80

Seafood Strata with Pesto 80

Dipping Sauce for Seafood 82

Seafood And Cabbage Salad 82

Lemon Seafood Risotto 82

Rachel's Crockpot Seafood Cheese Dip 83

Seafood Pasta Delight 84

Christmas Seafood Soup 84

Seafood Nachos 85

Banana Leaf Seafood 85

Seafood Chowder 86

Linguine with Seafood and Sundried Tomatoes 87

Campbell's Kitchen Seafood Bisque 87

Seafood Tomato Alfredo 88

A Simple Seafood Bisque 88

Seafood Salad Supreme 89

Ben's Seafood Dip 89

Mediterranean Seafood Salad 90

Chunky Seafood Sauce 90

Seafood Lasagna I 91

Cajun Seafood Pasta 91

Part 2 93

1. Baked Mussels And Cockles 94

2. Garlic-Butter Cockles 96

3. Crab Cakes 97

4. Herb Steamed Cockles 99

5. Crab Cakes With Lemon Aioli 100

6. Crab Cakes Benedict 102

7. Crab And Asparagus Frittata 104
8. Avocado King Crab Shooters 106
9. Grilled Snow Crab Legs 107
10. Spicy Crab Stuffed Cucumber Cups 108
11. Crab Stuffed Mushrooms 109
12. Grilled Crab In A Garlic-Herb-Butter 110
13. Sichuan Crawfish 111
14. Steamed King Crab Legs 113
15. Steamed Thai Clams 114
16. Stuffed "Poo Cha" Crab 115
17. Garlic-Butter-Herb Crawfish Tails 117
18. Southern Boiled Crawfish 119
19. French Langoustine (Large Prawns) 121
20. Lemon-Butter Lobster Tails 122
21. Thai Steamed Mussels 123
22. Broiled Bacon Wrapped Oysters 124
23. Crayfish And Spaghetti Squash Tagliatelle 125
24. Garlic Butter Mussels 127
25. Charbroiled Oysters 128
26. Pico de Gallo Grilled Oysters 130
27. Oysters Rockefeller 131
28. Half Shelled Oysters With Cucumber Mignonette 133
29. Baked Oysters 134
30. Lemon-Squeezed Seared Sea Scallops 135
Onion Bombs 136
Crispy Bacon Grilled Cheese Roll Ups 137
Greek Grilled Chicken 137

Grilled Zucchini Pizza Slices 139
Grilled Pork Chops & Sweet Potato Wedges 140
Grilled Vegetable Stack with Lemon Hummus 142
Grilled Soy & Honey Mustard Vegetables............................... 144
Grilled Vegetables with Chickpeas and Creamy Polenta 145
Easy Grilled Vegetables.. 146
Vietnamese Style Grilled Lemongrass Pork 148
Grilled Corn.. 149
Rosemary Shrimp Skewers with Arugula-White Bean Salad
.... 151
Pork & Veggie Kebabs... 153
Grilled Italian Flank Steak Pinwheels 155
Grilled Rainbow Carrots with basil vinaigrette..................... 157
Asian Grilled and Glazed Chicken Skewers 159
Grilled Pineapple Chicken Sandwich...................................... 161
Lemon Parmesan Foil-Pack Broccoli....................................... 163
Grilled Avocado with Melted Cheese & Hot Sauce 164
Cheddar Bacon BBQ Grilled Potatoes..................................... 165
Garlic Rubbed Roasted Cabbage Steaks 166
Grilled Corn Fritters 167
Eggs On the Grill 168
Grilled Seafood Packs with Lemon-Chive Butter.................. 169
Grill Broiled Sirloin Steak 171
Grill Chicken With Havana Sauce 171
Grill Poached Salmon 173
Grilled 'napalm' Shrimp... 173
Grilled Acorn Squash~ Mushroom & Asparagus................... 175

Grilled Angel Food Cake With Nectarines & Blu 176
Grilled Apple-Nut Stuffed Pork Chops 177
Grilled Asian-Spiced Mango & Chicken 178
Grilled Asparagus & Ginger-Lemon Vinaigrette 180
Grilled Asparagus With Lemon Dip 181
Grilled Balsamic Veal Chops 182
Grilled Bananas 183
Grilled Barbeque Chicken Breasts 183
Grilled Beef Blade Steaks With Spicy Orange 184
Grilled Beef Kabobs 185
Grilled Beef Tenderloin With Red Wine & Pis 186
Grilled Blue Cheese Slices 187
Grilled Bluefish Wrapped In Mammoth Basil Leaf 188

Part 1

Antoine's Oysters Rockefeller

Ingredients:

1/2 cup of bread crumbs
2 cups of freshly chopped spinach or 2 packs of (10-oz) frozen spinach
1/2 cup of parsley
1/2 cup of diced celery
2 tablespoons of diced onion
1 tablespoon of Pernod liqueur or anisette
1/4 teaspoon of salt
3 drops of Tabasco
18 large oysters
6 tablespoons of butter

Directions:

1. Melt the butter in a pan. Then add crumbs and sauté for 1 minute while stirring constantly.
2. Combine with other ingredients, with the exception of the oysters, and then blend in a blender until smooth.
3. Arrange oysters in shells (or individual dishes).
4. Top each oyster with 1 tablespoon of spinach mixture and broil for 3-5 minutes or until lightly browned.
5. Serve.

Artichoke Bottoms with Bay Scallops

Ingredients:

3/4 lb. of scallops, bay, washed
1 cup of bread crumbs, fresh, fine
3 tablespoon of parsley, fresh, minced
1/2 teaspoon of tarragon, dried
1/4 cup of celery, minced
2 cloves of garlic, minced
28 oz of artichoke bottoms, drained
1 cup of canola oil, for brushing

Directions:

1. First, mix the scallops, bread crumbs, parsley, tarragon, celery and garlic in a bowl.
2. Next, gently mound filling into artichoke bottoms.
3. Fire up your grill. When the coals are hot, set artichokes on grill rack and brush them with oil.
4. Set them about 4 to 6 inches from heat source. Cover the grill.
5. Next, cook stuffed artichokes for about 3 minutes or until the scallops are opaque.
6. Using a long-handled spatula, transfer the artichoke bottoms to the serving dish.
7. Serve while still hot.

Art's Mock Crabmeat Casserole

Ingredients:

1 cup of mayonnaise

1 cup of sour cream

2 tablespoons of parsley

1 tablespoon of onion; diced

1 green pepper, diced

1 teaspoon of curry powder

6 hard-boiled eggs, chopped

1 lb. of mock crabmeat

1 paprika

Directions:

1. Combine all the listed ingredients, with the exception of the paprika.
2. Next, pour them into a well-greased 1 1/2-quart casserole.
3. Next, sprinkle paprika all over the surface.
4. Place in the oven and bake at 350 F for around 40 to 50 minutes.
5. Serve over hot, cooked rice.

Avocado Crabmeat Salad

Ingredients:

1 lb. of crabmeat

2 tablespoons of mayonnaise

3 tablespoon pickapepper sauce

1/4 lb. of jalapeno cheese -- grated

1/4 lb. of cheddar cheese -- grated

8 hearts of palm

8 artichoke hearts

1 basket of cherry tomatoes

1 large ripe avocado -- in 1/8's

2 hard-boiled eggs

1 lettuce

1 lemon wedge

Directions:

1. First, mix all the above ingredients together.
2. Add a little oil from the artichokes as you mix.
3. Chill and serve on lettuce with lemon slices.

Bacon And Smoked Oysters

Ingredients:

2 cans of smoked oysters

1/4 cup of light vegetable oil

1/2 lb. of bacon strips

40 round wooden toothpicks

3 tablespoons of garlic, minced

Directions:

1. First, slice up the bacon strips in thirds.
2. Next, wrap a bacon slice around each oyster and place a toothpick through the middle in order to hold it in place.
3. In a medium skillet, heat oil, and add garlic.
4. Next, cook the wrapped oysters in the warm oil until the bacon is crisp.
5. Remove from pan and set aside to drain on a paper towel.
6. Serve.

Bailey's Bouillabaisse (Fish Stew)

Ingredients:

1 large onion, diced
2 cups of celery, diced
3 potatoes, small, diced
3 cups of boiling water
2 cups of skimmed milk
1 1/2 lbs. of cod or flounder
2 cups of broccoli, diced
2 cups of cauliflower, diced
1 1/2 teaspoons of salt
1/2 teaspoons of pepper
1/2 teaspoon of marjoram
1/2 teaspoon of basil

Directions:

1. First, boil the onion, celery, and potatoes in the water for about 10 minutes.
2. Mix a little bit of the milk with the flour to form a soupy paste and set aside for later use.
3. Next, add the remaining ingredients and apply heat and bring to a boil.
4. Add the flour mixture while stirring constantly.
5. Allow to simmer for roughly 15 to 20 minutes.
6. Serve.

Baked Clams With Black Bean Sauce

Ingredients:

24 clams

1 tablespoon of sesame oil

2 teaspoons of ginger, fresh; finely grated

2 teaspoons of garlic; minced

1/2 teaspoon of red pepper flakes

1/4 cup of fermented black beans; rinsed & mashed

2 tablespoons of white wine

1 tablespoon of soy sauce

3 tablespoons of scallion; chopped

Directions:

1. First, shuck the clams and place them on a baking sheet. Set aside for later use.
2. Mix the remaining ingredients in a small saucepan. Apply medium heat and bring to boil.
3. Spoon the mixture on top of the mollusks. Place in the oven and proceed to bake for 5 to 7 minutes at a temperature of 450 degrees Fahrenheit or until cooked but not tough.
4. Serve.

Baked Crab Quesadillas

Ingredients:
1/3 cup of unsalted butter or margarine
1/4 cup of vegetable oil
1/2 cup of chopped onion
2 jalapeno pepper, seeded
1 centiliter garlic, minced
1 lb. of lump crabmeat, drained
1/4 cup of mayonnaise
1 tablespoon of chopped fresh cilantro
1 teaspoon of salt
16 8-inch flour tortillas
1/3 cup of shredded Monterey jack
1 cup of cheese with jalapeno peppers

Directions:

1. First, mix the butter and oil. Set them aside for later.

2. Next, sauté the onions, peppers, and garlic in 2 tbsp. of the reserved butter mixture in a medium-sized saucepan. Apply medium high heat while stirring constantly, until they become tender.

3. Remove saucepan from the heat. Proceed to stir in crabmeat gently and then add the mayonnaise, fresh cilantro, shredded Monterey jack and salt.

4. Place the tortillas on a baking sheets and brush 1 side of each tortilla, and sprinkle with cheese.

5. Fold them in half.

6. Place them in the oven and bake at 475 degrees for 4 minutes or until golden brown.

7. Cut each tortilla into thirds and serve warm.

Baked Salmon Steaks

Ingredients:

6 salmon steaks, 1 inch thick

1/3 cup of butter or margarine

1/2 teaspoon of salt

1/4 teaspoon of paprika

1 teaspoon of Worcestershire sauce

2 tablespoons of grated onion

Directions:

1. Preheat the oven to a temperature of 350 degrees Fahrenheit.
2. Next, position the salmon steaks in a well-greased shallow baking dish.
3. Melt the butter, add seasonings and Worcestershire sauce. Next, spread this mixture over the fish.
4. Proceed to sprinkle one tsp. of the grated onion over each steak.
5. Transfer to the oven and bake with moderate heat for about 25 to 30 minutes.
6. Remove from oven and serve.

Barbecue Crab Sandwich

Ingredients:

1 cup of crab

1/2 cup of tomato sauce

1/4 cup of green stuffed olives; sliced

8 oz. of cheddar; cut in small cubes

8 English muffins

Directions:

1. First, combine all the ingredients except the English muffins together in a bowl.
2. Transfer to the refrigerator and allow to refrigerate for at least 1 hour to blend the flavors.
3. Next, spread it on the English muffin halves and broil until hot and cheese is melted.
4. Serve hot.

Barbecued Catfish

Ingredients:

6 catfish; lb. each
1/8 teaspoon of paprika
1/4 teaspoon of salt
1/4 teaspoon of pepper
2 tablespoons of sugar
1 teaspoon of Worcestershire sauce
1/4 cup of vinegar
1/4 cup of catsup
1/2 cup of vegetable oil

Directions:

1. First, wash and clean the fish very well. Next, skin and fillet the fish.
2. Next, mix together all the remaining ingredients.
3. Baste the fish with the prepared sauce.
4. Next, place the fish in a well-greased, hinged fish basket.
5. Position this on a grill at a distance of about 3 to 4 inches from the coals.
6. Proceed to cook the fish for about 7 to 8 minutes on each side or until fish flakes easily, while brushing frequently with the sauce.
7. Remove from the grill and serve.

Barbecued Salmon With Basil

Ingredients:

4 salmon steaks (6 to 8 ounces each); thawed

2 tablespoons of lemon juice

2 tablespoons of olive oil

1 teaspoon of dried and crushed basil

1 lemon wedge

Directions:

1. Mix the lemon juice, olive oil and basil together. Next, brush this mixture on both sides of the salmon.
2. Grill over medium hot coals for 10 minutes per inch of thickness or until fish flakes when tested with a fork.
3. Remove from the grill when the fish is done.
4. Serve with lemon wedges.

Basic Best Salmon Loaf

Ingredients:

15 1/2 oz of canned Alaska salmon

2 cups of soft bread crumbs

1/3 cup of finely minced onions

1/4 cup of milk

2 eggs

2 tablespoons of chopped parsley

1 tablespoon of lemon juice

1/4 teaspoon of dill weeds

1 dash of black pepper

Directions:

1. First, drain and flake the salmon, while reserving 2 tablespoons of liquid for later use.
2. Mix the flaked salmon and the reserved liquid with the remaining ingredients.
3. Place this mixture in a well-greased medium-sized loaf pan or shape into loaf on a greased baking pan.
4. Place in an oven and bake at 350 degrees for about 45 minutes.
5. Remove from oven and serve.

Basque Style Steamed Clams

Ingredients:

4 quarts of cherrystone clams

4 cloves of garlic, minced

1 onion, minced

1 tablespoon of parsley, minced

1 tablespoon of olive oil

1/2 cup of dry white wine

1/2 cup of water

1/4 teaspoon of black pepper, freshly ground

Directions:

1. Wash all of the clams carefully and place them in a large kettle.
2. Next, add the remaining ingredients into the kettle.
3. Cover the kettle and cook over medium heat for an estimated 20 minutes.
4. Serve hot in individual bowls, accompanied by green salad and slices of French bread.

Brigitte's Shrimp Or Tuna Mousse

Ingredients:

2 tablespoons of mayonnaise
1/2 cup of water
1 can of tomato soup
1 pack of 8 oz cream cheese
1 teaspoon of paprika
1 lb. shrimp or 2 small cans of tuna
1/4 cup of peppers, finely chopped
1/2 cup of celery, finely chopped
1 tablespoon of onion, grated
1 teaspoon of Worcestershire sauce
1/4 teaspoon of salt
1 pack of unflavored gelatin
1 cup of water

Directions:

1. First, soak the gelatin in water.
2. Next, heat the undiluted soup; add gelatin and stir well until dissolved.
3. Proceed to mash the cream cheese, add to the soup and continue to apply heat until the cheese is totally dissolved.
4. Allow to cool down. Next, fold in the mayonnaise, shrimp or tuna, and vegetables and seasonings.
5. Mix well and put into a well-oiled mould.

Brigitte's Tuna Burgers

Ingredients:

6 slices of turkey bacon

1 egg

2 cans of 7 oz. tuna (not drained)

6 tomato slices

1 teaspoon of mustard

1/3 cup of low fat mayonnaise

1 tablespoon of minced onion

6 hamburger buns

Directions:

1. The first step is to cook the bacon. When that is done, set it aside and proceed to beat the egg in a suitable container.
2. Next, into the beaten egg, add tuna, mustard, mayonnaise, onion, bread crumbs, and mix well.
3. Spoon this mixture onto the bottom halves of buns.
4. Broil them at a distance of 6 inches away from the heat till they brown. This should take about six minutes.
5. Next, top each one with a tomato slice and two pieces of cooked bacon. Cover with the top of buns which have been toasted lightly.
6. Serve.

Broiled Bay Scallops

Ingredients:

1 lb. of bay scallops or sea scallops halved

1 teaspoon of paprika

Pepper; to taste

Juice of 1 lemon

2 tablespoons of parsley; chopped fresh

Directions:

1. First, preheat the broiler and wash and rinse the scallops very carefully. Set aside to dry.
2. Place them in a suitable baking dish.
3. Next, season them with paprika and pepper on all sides.
4. Sprinkle with lemon juice.
5. Next, broil the scallops keeping them about 3 inches away from the heat source for 3 minutes. Broil them until they turn opaque.
6. Turn them over to make sure that they are cooked through.
7. Garnish with parsley.
8. Serve.

Broiled Fish With Devilled Cheese

Ingredients:

2 lb. of fish fillets

½ cup of butter; melted

1 cup of cheddar; shredded

2 tablespoons of chili sauce

1 tablespoon of mustard; prepared

1 1/2 teaspoons of horseradish; prepared

Directions:

1. First, position the fish fillets on a buttered broiler pan.
2. Next, brush the fillets with the melted butter and broil for about 8 to 10 minutes or until the fish flakes easily with a fork.
3. Mix all of the remaining ingredients and blend them together well.
4. Next, spoon this mixture onto the fish fillets and broil for another 2 to 4 minutes or until the cheddar begins to melt and is browned lightly.
5. Serve.

Broiled Monkfish In Gingered Soy Sauce

Ingredients:

4 fillets of monkfish

1/2 cup of light soy sauce

1 minced garlic clove

1 tablespoon of grated fresh ginger

1 white pepper to taste

Directions:

1. First, mix together the soy sauce, garlic, ginger and pepper in a suitable container.
2. Marinate the monkfish in this mixture for several hours in the refrigerator, while turning it only once.
3. Next, remove from the refrigerator and transfer the fish to a broiler pan. Proceed to broil the fish for about 8-10 minutes until fish flakes easily with a fork.
4. Serve fish with brown rice and a green vegetable.

Broiled Seafood Canapés

Ingredients:

1 cup of cooked seafood, flaked

6 slices of white bread

1/4 cup of butter

1/4 cup of cheddar or 1/3 cup of ketchup

1 American cheese, grated

Directions:

1. The first step is to toast the bread slices on one side and then trim off crusts. Once that is done, cut bread in half.
2. Next, butter up the untoasted sides of the bread slices; cover this with a layer of seafood, then ketchup and top up with cheese.
3. Place canapés on a baking sheet under the broiler.
4. Broil until the cheese is melted and the canapés are heated through.
5. Serve.

Broken Fish Trap Soup

Ingredients:

2 cups of fish stock
2 lime leaves
1 lemon grass piece
1/2 teaspoon of ginger
3 tablespoons of nouk mam (Vietnamese fish)
1 lemon
1/4 lb. of shrimp
1/4 lb. of oysters
1/4 lb. of crab meat
1/4 lb. of fish pieces
1/4 lb. of scallops
3/4 cup of coconut milk
3 red chili peppers, crushed

Directions:

1. First, chop the lime leaves. And extract the juice from the lemon.

2. Next, apply heat to the fish stock and then add lime leaves, lemon grass, ginger, Nook Mam & lemon juice.

3. Bring to a low boil while stirring.

4. Next, add the seafood & coconut milk.

5. Simmer at just below boiling until the seafood is cooked, while stirring constantly.

6. Next, add the chili peppers and stir.

7. Serve with lime wedges and steamed rice.

Butterfish With Lemongrass

Ingredients:

1 tablespoon of vegetable oil

2 lb. of butterfish or other fillets

1 1/2 tablespoons of vinegar

1 tablespoon of thin sliced fresh lemongrass

1 fresh jalapeno, chopped

1 pinch of sugar

1/2 cup of water

Directions:

1. Pour the vegetable oil in a frying pan and apply medium heat.
2. Next, add the fish first and then followed by the other ingredients.
3. Allow to simmer while uncovered for 10 minutes while spooning the pan juices all over the fish frequently.
4. Remove from the pan and serve.

Cajun Fish Fillets

Ingredients:

3 tablespoons of butter

1 tablespoon of Cajun's choice blackened sea

1 tablespoon of minced garlic

1/4 cup of vermouth of white wine

4 lemon wedges

1 lb. of fish fillets

Directions:

1. First, you need to melt the butter in a pan over medium-high heat.
2. Next, stir in 1 tablespoon of Cajun's Choice and minced garlic and stir constantly for two minutes to cook the garlic.
3. Stop the butter and minced garlic from cooking any further by adding Vermouth or white wine.
4. Stir constantly and cook for 1 minute.
5. Next, add the fish fillets and cook them until the fish flakes apart.
6. Next, squeeze the lemon wedges all over the fish.
7. Serve.

California-Style Salmon

Ingredients:

4 8-10 oz. of salmon steaks

1 cup of ripe olives -- chopped

1/2 cup of chopped tomatoes

1/4 cup of chopped onions

1 tablespoon of vegetable oil

1 tablespoon of fresh cilantro -- minced

1 teaspoon of garlic -- minced

Directions:

1. First, grill the salmon while being careful to not overcook them.
2. Next, mix the olives, tomato, onions, cilantro, oil and garlic together in a medium-sized bowl.
3. Serve the grilled fish with the prepared mixture.
4. Garnish with even more cilantro if desired.

Camp Tuna & Rice

Ingredients:

2 cans of tuna (and the fluid too)

1 cup of quick-cooking brown rice

2 tablespoons of instant dried onions

2 tablespoons of green pepper flakes

1 3/4 cups of boiling water

Directions:

1. First, heat the tuna in its oil in a medium-sized skillet.
2. Next, add the remaining listed ingredients into the skillet and bring to a boil.
3. Cover and cook for about 15 to 20 minutes.
4. Serve.

Catfish Chilli

Ingredients:

2 lb. of catfish fillets, chunked

1 cup of chopped green pepper

2 tablespoons of butter

2 cloves of minced garlic

1 1/2 teaspoons of salt

1 lb. of red kidney beans

1 lb. of canned tomatoes, not drained

6 oz of tomato paste

Directions:

1. Sauté the green pepper and garlic in butter until they are tender.
2. Add seasonings and stir them together. Next, add the beans as well as the tomatoes.
3. Cover and allow to simmer for about 15 minutes.
4. Next, add the fish and cover. Let it simmer for an extra 15 minutes or until the fish flakes easily.
5. Serve.

Catfish Mexican Style

Ingredients:

4 catfish fillets

16 oz of picante sauce

6 Monterey jack cheese, grated

Directions:

1. Place all the catfish fillets in a suitable microwave dish and cover it up while leaving a vent.
2. Next, microwave it on high heat for 10 minutes while rotating dish occasionally.
3. Uncover the dish and sprinkle the contents with grated cheese.
4. Proceed to microwave it again while uncovered for 30 seconds or until cheese is melted.
5. Serve.

Cheer Up A Crab

Ingredients:

2 10 ounce packages of frozen spinach (cooked and well drained)
1 10 ounce can of rootle tomatoes and green chilies
1 cup of sour cream
1 cup of grated cheese
1 cup of crabmeat (canned, fresh or frozen)
1/2 teaspoon of nutmeg
1/2 teaspoon of Mrs. Dash
1 teaspoon of dill weed
2 tablespoons of chopped onion

Directions:

1. First, place all the spinach in greased casserole dish.
2. Mix all the other ingredients together in a suitable container. Stir very well
3. Pour out this mixture all over the spinach.
4. Transfer the casserole dish to the oven and bake at 350 degrees Fahrenheit for about 25 to 30 minutes.
5. Remove from the oven and serve.

Cheesy Broiled Flounder

Ingredients:

2 lb. of flounder or white fish
2 tablespoons of lemon juice
1/2 cup of parmesan cheese
1/4 cup of butter, softened
3 tablespoons of mayonnaise
3 green onions, chopped
1/4 teaspoon of salt
1 dash of hot sauce
Parsley (optional, to garnish if desired)
Lemon twists (optional, to garnish if desired)

Directions:

1. Stack the fillets in a single layer on a greased, shallow oven-to-table type broiler pan. Brush with the lemon juice.
2. Next, mix the rest of the ingredients together in a suitable container and set aside for later use.
3. Broil the fillets for 4 to 6 minutes or until fish flakes easily when tested with a fork.
4. Next, remove from oven then spread the prepared cheese mixture over it.
5. Broil for an extra 30 seconds or until cheese is lightly browned and bubbly.
6. Next, garnish with lemon twists and parsley if desired.
7. Serve.

Cheesy Salmon Supper

Ingredients:

1 tablespoon of lemon juice
2 eggs, beaten
1 cup of rolled oats
1 cup of cheese, grated
1/4 cup of onion, diced
1/2 cup of celery, diced
1/2 cup of carrots, grated
1/2 teaspoon of salt
1/8 teaspoon of pepper
1/2 teaspoon of parsley flakes, dried
1 can of cream of mushroom soup (8oz)
3/4 cup of milk
2 cans of Salmon (7 ¾ oz. cans)

Directions:

1. Using a suitable container, mix all the listed ingredients together (with the exception of the mushroom soup and milk).
2. Next, transfer the mixture to an oven and bake in a casserole dish at 350 degrees for 40 to 45 minutes.
3. Remove from oven.
4. Mix the mushroom soup and milk together. Heat gently and pour over the loaf as a sauce.
5. Serve.

Chile Tuna Sea Shells

Ingredients:

6 green chilies (skinned, seeds removed, chopped)
2 tablespoons of prepared chili sauce
1 can of white tuna (drained and flaked)
1/4 cup mayonnaise
2 teaspoons of prepared horseradish sauce
4 green onions (chopped)
1/4 cup of green olives (sliced)
1/2 lb. of sea shell macaroni
1 avocado (peeled, pit removed, chopped)
2 sprigs of cilantro (chopped)

Directions:

1. First, cook the macaroni in sufficient amount of salted water until it is just done but yet still firm. Drain and rinse in cold water.
2. Next, mix all the other ingredients, except the avocado and cilantro. Set aside this mixture for at least two hours to blend the flavors together.
3. Next, garnish with the avocado and cilantro and serve.

Chinese Oyster Stew

Ingredients:

1 can (10 ¾ ounces) of condensed chicken broth
1 soup can water
2 tablespoons of soy sauce
1/4 teaspoon of grated gingerroot
1 pinch of shucked large oysters (not drained)
2 cups of chopped Chinese cabbage
8 ounces of sliced mushrooms
1/2 cup of bean sprouts
4 green onions (with tops), cut into 1-inch pieces

Directions:

1. First, apply heat to the broth, water, soy sauce and gingerroot to boiling in a 3-quart saucepan.
2. Add oysters, cabbage, mushrooms and bean sprouts into the pan.
3. Next, heat mixture till it boils and then reduce the heat. Cover and simmer for about 2 minutes or until cabbage is cook.
4. Finally, ladle the stew into bowls and garnish with green onions.
5. Serve.

Coconut Fish Roe Samba

Ingredients:

1 Stephen ceideburg

1 cup of desiccated or freshly grated coconut

1 oz. of fish roe (chopped)

1/4 teaspoon of turmeric

2 teaspoons of ground chili

1 lemon (the juice only)

2 oz. of hot water (to moisten the coconut)

1 onion (grated)

1-inch piece ginger (scraped and grated)

Salt to taste

Directions:

1. Mix all ingredients together in a saucepan.
2. Next, cook on low heat for about 20 minutes with the lid on the saucepan.
3. Stir occasionally to prevent it from burning.
4. Remove from the heat source and serve.

Codfish Vegetable Casserole

Ingredients:

1/4 cup of chopped onion

2 cups of white sauce

1/4 teaspoon of paprika

1 cup of corn kernels

1 tablespoon of butter

1/2 teaspoon of pepper

2 cups of flaked codfish (fresh)

1 cup of cooked vegetables

Directions:

1. First, fry the chopped onions in the butter until they are tender.
2. Next, add the other listed ingredients and season with salt to taste.
3. Next, pour the mixture into a greased casserole dish and cover with pastry dough.
4. Transfer to the oven and bake at a temperature of 425 degrees Fahrenheit for half an hour.
5. Remove from the oven and serve.

Confetti Crab Salad

Ingredients:

1 lb. of crab meat (with shells and cartilage removed)

1/2 cup of mayonnaise

1/2 cup of finely chopped radishes

2 tablespoons of finely chopped fresh parsley

2 tablespoons of finely chopped onion or scallions

2 tablespoons of drained capers (finely chopped)

1 tablespoon of lemon juice

1/2 teaspoon of salt

1/8 teaspoon of freshly ground black pepper

Directions:

1. First, using a suitable bowl, mix all of the listed ingredients together.
2. Place the bowl in the refrigerator and refrigerate until serving time.
3. Remove from refrigerator and serve.

Crab And Corn Cakes

Ingredients:

1 cup of corn

2 cloves of garlic, chopped

1 teaspoon of Dijon mustard

1 egg

1 teaspoon of Worcestershire sauce

1/2 cup of crab

1/2 cup of flour

2 green onions, chopped

Directions:
1. First, put 1/2 cup of corn, garlic, Worcestershire sauce, mustard and egg in a blender and blend together until it is smooth.
2. Next, add the leftover corn, crab, onions and enough flour to make a thick mixture.
3. Proceed to fry the mixture in a skillet.
4. Serve.

    P. S – If you wish to make this recipe have low-fat and high fiber, use 2 egg whites instead of whole egg and also use oat flakes instead of flour.

Crab Broccoli Casserole

Ingredients:

1 bunch of broccoli
2 tablespoons of butter
1/2 lb. of crab meat
1 cup of sour cream
1 tablespoon of grated lemon peel
2 tablespoons of lemon juice
1/4 cup of chili sauce
1 cup of cheddar cheese (grated)
1 small onion (diced)
1 dash of sea salt
1 dash of cayenne

Directions:

1. Sauté the broccoli in butter until it is tender. Then, cut them up into small pieces.
2. Next, mix the broccoli with crab meat.
3. Add the remaining ingredients and stir.
4. Next, pour the mixture into a small oiled baking dish and place in the oven.
5. Proceed to bake it while uncovered at 350 degrees for 20 minutes, or until cheese is melted and top becomes brown.
6. Remove from oven and serve.

Crabs With Ginger & Green Onions

Ingredients:

4 tablespoons of peanut oil
2 lb. of live, unshelled, crab (cleaned)
2 tablespoons of minced garlic
1 teaspoon of minced fresh ginger root
4 tablespoons of coarsely chopped scallions
2 tablespoons of Chinese rice wine or dry sherry
2 tablespoons of light soy sauce
1/2 teaspoon of dark soy sauce
1 pinch of salt
1/4 cup of chicken broth

Directions:

1. First step is to heat a wok over a high flame.
2. Next, add the peanut oil, and when it is hot, stir-fry the crab quickly until they turn red.
3. Add the remaining ingredients.
4. Continue stirring until the crabs are cooked. This should take about 3 minutes.
5. Serve.

Crawfish Chilli

Ingredients:
2 lbs. of lean ground beef
2 lbs. of crawfish tails
1 teaspoon of garlic, chopped fine
2 teaspoons of salt
1 tablespoon of soy sauce
1 teaspoon of cayenne pepper
1 teaspoon of dried mint
1 tablespoon of dried parsley
3 tablespoons of chili powder
1 can of (8 oz) tomato sauce
1 cup of dry white wine
1 cup of water
1 teaspoon of lemon or lime juice
1 cup of chopped onions
1 bacon drippings

Directions:

1. First, brown the ground beef in the bacon drippings.
2. Next, mix all other ingredients with meat. Apply heat and bring to a boil.
3. Allow to simmer for a few hours.
4. Serve.

Cream Of Crab Soup

Ingredients:

1 lb. of crabmeat

1/4 teaspoon of celery salt

1 chicken bouillon cube

1 cup of boiling water

1 dash of pepper

1/4 cup of chopped onion

1 quart of milk

1 cup of butter

1 chopped parsley

3 tablespoons of flour

Directions:

1. First, melt the chicken bouillon cube in water.
2. Next, cook the onion in butter until they are tender. Blend in flour and seasonings.
3. Add milk and chicken bouillon solution gradually and cook while stirring constantly until it becomes thick.
4. Next, add the crabmeat and apply heat.
5. Next, garnish with parsley and serve.

Creamed Lobster & Clams

Ingredients:

2 green onions, sliced
3 tablespoons of butter
3 tablespoons of flour
1/2 teaspoon of salt
1/8 teaspoon of cayenne
1 1/2 cups half and half (cream & milk)
3 tablespoon of dry white wine
1/2 cup of cooked lobster
1/2 cup of cooked clams, minced pastry shells
1 can of mushrooms (4 ½ oz., drained)

Directions:

1. In a saucepan, sauté the green onions in butter until tender.
2. Next, stir in the flour, salt and cayenne into the pan.
3. Next, add the half and half milk into the pan at once.
4. Proceed to cook the mixture while stirring constantly, until the mixture is thick and bubbly.
5. Now, add the wine, clams, lobster and button mushrooms.
6. Heat through and serve in warm pastry shells.

Creole Fish Soup

Ingredients:

1 lb. of red snapper (boned/shredded)

1 cup of minced onion

1 cup of cooked strained tomatoes

1 bay leaf

1 cayenne pepper

2 tablespoons of lemon juice

1 lb. of shelled shrimp, diced

1 cup of diced potatoes

1 tablespoon of butter or margarine

Salt to taste

6 cups of water

Directions:

1. Mix all the ingredients, except the lemon juice, in a large saucepan.
2. Next, allow to simmer for 40 minutes, or until vegetables are tender.
3. Add the lemon juice and stir.
4. Serve.

Devilled Crab Croquettes

Ingredients:

1 lb. of crabmeat

1/2 teaspoon of salt

1 cup of mashed potatoes

1 pack of old bay seasoning

2 eggs (hard boiled, chopped)

1 dash of onion powder

1 small green pepper, chopped

1 tablespoon of parsley, chopped

1 egg, beaten

1 cracker meal pack

Directions:

1. First, Sautee the chopped green pepper and parsley and set aside.
2. Mix the crabmeat, mashed potatoes, seasonings, chopped egg, green pepper and parsley, as well as the beaten egg.
3. Mould into croquettes; roll in cracker meal and deep fry until they turn golden brown.
4. Serve.

Firecracker Grilled Alaskan Salmon

Ingredients:

4 6-oz. of salmon steaks
1/4 cup of peanut oil
2 tablespoons of soy sauce
2 tablespoons of balsamic vinegar
2 tablespoons of chopped scallions
1 1/2 teaspoons of brown sugar
1 clove of garlic, minced
3/4 teaspoon of grated fresh ginger root
1/2 teaspoon of red chili flakes (or more to taste)
1/2 teaspoon of sesame oil
1/8 teaspoon of salt

Directions:

1. Place the salmon steaks in a glass dish.

2. Next, whisk all the remaining ingredients together and pour them over the salmon.

3. Cover this up with plastic wrap and marinate in the refrigerator for 4 to 6 hours.

4. Next, heat up your grill.

5. Remove the salmon from the marinade, brush the grill with oil and place the salmon on the grill.

6. Next, grill over medium heat for 10 minutes per inch of thickness, measured at the thickest part.

7. Turn it halfway through cooking. Cook until the fish just flakes when tested with a fork.

8. Remove from the grill and serve.

Fried Fish In Spicy Sauce

Ingredients:

1/4 cup of olive oil
1 1/2 lbs. of fish fillets
3/4 cup of water
2 carrots -- thinly sliced
2 small onions -- sliced
1 green pepper -- cut in ring
1 garlic clove -- minced
1 tablespoon packed brown sugar
1/2 teaspoon of salt
1/4 teaspoon of ground ginger
1/3 cup of cider vinegar
2 teaspoons of cornstarch

Directions:

1. First, cut the fish fillets into serving-sized pieces. Pat them dry.

2. Next, heat the oil in a skillet over medium heat.

3. Place the fish in the skillet and cook for 8-10 minutes or until the fish flakes easily with fork; turning carefully.

4. Next, heat water, carrots, onions, green pepper, garlic, brown sugar, salt and ginger to boiling point. Cover, reduce heat and cook for about 5 minutes.

5. Next, mix the vinegar and cornstarch; stir into the vegetables. Heat to boiling while stirring constantly.

6. Boil for about a minute, and then pour over fish.

7. Serve immediately.

Guianese Curried Fish

Ingredients:

1 lb. of fish fillets
1 pinch of salt
3 tablespoons of vinegar
1 pinch of saffron
1/2 teaspoon of peppercorns
1 teaspoon of dry mustard
1/4 cup of ghee or 3 tbsp. of vegetable oil
1 large onion, thinly sliced
2 large garlic cloves, crushed
2 medium red chili peppers, finely chopped

Directions:

1. Place the fish in an open pan. Add the salt andvinegar.
2. Cook the saffron, peppercorns and mustard in the heated ghee or vegetable oil until well mixed.
3. Pour this spice mixture over the fish in vinegar and cook for 15 minutes.
4. Next, add the onion, garlic and chilies with a little quantity of water. Cover and cook, slowly, for 25 minutes.
5. Serve.

Gorton's New England Clam Chowder

Ingredients:

2 cans of Gorton's clams

1 cup of pared diced potatoes

2 tablespoons of butter

1/4 cup of chopped onions

2 cups of milk

Salt and pepper to taste

Sherry (optional)

Directions:

1. First, drain the clams.
2. Next, cook the chopped onions in the butter.
3. Next, pour the potatoes and clam juice. Proceed to cook until tender.
4. Next, add the clams and milk to the mixture.
5. Apply heat and add the salt and pepper to your taste.

    P.S – Be careful not to let it boil.

Grilled Spiced Fish

Ingredients:

4 oz. of Sole (skinned)
2/3 cup of plain yogurt
2 teaspoons of garam masala
1 teaspoon of ground coriander
2 garlic cloves (crushed)
1/2 teaspoon of chili powder
1 tablespoon of lemon juice
1 lemon wedge for garnish
Salt and pepper to taste

Directions:

1. First, wash the fish properly and rinse. Next, pat dry the fish with paper towels and place in a shallow non-metal dish.
2. Season fish by sprinkling with salt and pepper.
3. Next, mix together the yogurt, coriander, chili powder, garlic, and lemon juice together in a suitable container.
4. Pour this mixture all over the fish. Cover and refrigerate 2 to 3 hours in order to allow fish to absorb flavors.
5. Next, preheat the broiler. Place the fish on the broiler rack and cook for about 8 minutes, until fish just begins to flake, while basting with cooking juices.
6. Turn over the fish halfway through cooking.
7. Serve hot, garnished with lemon wedges.

Henderson Boiled Crawfish

Ingredients:

25 lbs. of crawfish, live

Salt & pepper

3 gallons of water

2 cups of red pepper

1/2 black pepper

6 lemons, halved

6 onions, large, cut in 1/8th

1 potato and corn, pre-boiled

Directions:

1. First, pour the water in a suitable pan/pot and add pepper and salt. Bring the solution to a boil.
2. Next, add crawfish into the water solution and bring to a boil again.
3. Add the onions, lemon, potatoes and corn.
4. Apply heat again and cook for no more than 10 minutes.
5. Remove the crawfish and do not let it soak.

Herbs & Trout

Ingredients:

2 8-10 oz. trout

4 tablespoons of melted butter

1 lemon; sliced

1 orange; sliced

Salt and pepper; to taste

Basil to taste

Thyme to taste

1 shallot; to taste

1 dash of paprika

Directions:

1. Brush the trout all over with melted butter.
2. Next, season them with the salt, pepper, basil, thyme and shallots.
3. Place the lemon and orange slices on top of the trout in an alternating pattern.
4. Next, sprinkle with a dash of paprika.
5. Next, proceed to steam them over clear water for around 7-10 minutes.
6. Remove and serve.

Hickory Smoked Salmon

Ingredients:

6 4-6 oz. of salmon fillets

2 teaspoons of dark brown sugar

1 seafood seasoning – to taste

Directions:

1. First, spread wet hickory chips over hot coals.
2. Place each fillet on a greased grill or skewer and place them on a raised rack.
3. Next, spread dark brown sugar over the salmon and sprinkle with seafood seasoning.
4. Cover up the grill and cook for 20 minutes or until fish flakes easily when tested with a fork.
5. Remove from the grill and serve.

High Country Fried Trout

Ingredients:

2 trout, fresh

1/2 cup of plain flour

Cooking oil

Directions:

1. First, pour out a small quantity of cooking oil in a suitable pan and heat.
2. Next, wash and clean the trout thoroughly. Roll them in flour and place them in the pan.
3. Place the pan on a heat source and cook for 3 to 4 minutes on each side.
4. Remove from the pan and serve.

Oriental Steamed Fish

Ingredients:

4 white fish steaks (about 3/4 thick)
1 tablespoon of slivered fresh ginger root
1/4 cup of orange juice
2 tablespoons of soy sauce
1 1/2 teaspoons of distilled white vinegar
1/2 teaspoon of brown sugar
1 teaspoon of sesame oil
2 green onions and tops (minced)

Directions:

1. Place the fish, in single layer, on oiled rack of bamboo steamer. Spread the ginger evenly all over the fish.
2. Next, set the rack in large pot or wok of boiling water (do not let the water make contact with the fish).
3. Cover and steam for about 8 to 10 minutes, or until the fish flakes easily when tested with fork.
4. Next, mix the orange juice, soy sauce, vinegar and brown sugar together in a small pan.
5. Apply heat and bring the mixture to boil.
6. Remove from the heat source and stir in the sesame oil.
7. Next, arrange the fish on a serving platter. Sprinkle green onions over the fish and pour the sauce over everything.

Oysters Annapolis

Ingredients:

24 oysters, shucked
1/3 cup of mayonnaise
3 teaspoons of Worcestershire sauce
2 egg yolks
1 salt
1/2 cup green bell pepper, cored
Ground pepper
12 oz. of crabmeat; with 1 shell only
1 clove of garlic; chopped
3 tablespoons of cracker crumbs
1 teaspoon of dry mustard

Directions:

1. First, preheat the oven to a temperature of 350 degrees.
2. Next, cut up the oysters into several pieces.
3. Place them in the half shells. Place those on a baking sheet.
4. Next, mix the remaining ingredients together in a small bowl.
5. Toss them together gently. Proceed to pile the mixture on top of the oysters.
6. Transfer to the preheated oven and bake for 20 to 25 minutes.
7. Remove from the oven and serve hot.

Pacific Clam & Corn Chowder

Ingredients:

8 oz. of minced clams
1 cup of clam nectar and water
3 slices of bacon, chopped
1 cup of chopped onions
2 cups of diced raw potatoes
1 1/2 cups of drained whole kernel corn
3 cups of milk
2 tablespoons of flour
1 tablespoon of butter
1 teaspoon of celery salt
1 teaspoon of salt
1 dash of white pepper
1/2 cup coarse cracker crumbs (optional)

Directions:

1. Drain the clams and reserve the liquid for future use.

2. Next, add water to the clam liquid to make it up to 1 cup.

3. Fry the bacon in a suitable pan until they are crisp. Add the onions and cook until tender.
4. Next, add the potatoes and nectar-water. Cover and allow to simmer gently until potatoes are tender. Add corn and milk.

5. Next, blend the flour and butter and stir into chowder. Cook slowly until the mixture thickens slightly, while stirring constantly.

6. Add the seasonings and clams and simmer for five minutes.

7. Serve hot and top with cracker crumbs.

Penne Pasta With Tuna

Ingredients:
1 can (7 oz.) of tuna; drained - optional
1/2 cup of walnuts
1 lemon rind
1 teaspoon of Worcestershire sauce
1/4 cup of chopped parsley
4 fresh basil leaves
1/2 cup of olive oil
1/2 teaspoon of salt
1/4 teaspoon of pepper
1 lb. of penne pasta

Directions:

1. Pour out the tuna, walnuts, lemon rind, Worcestershire sauce, parsley, basil, oil, salt, and pepper into a food processor or blender.
2. Cover up the ingredients and process or blend until smooth.
3. Cook the pasta according to package directions. Drain the pasta.
4. Next, stir in the tuna mixture, coating pasta with sauce.
5. Serve immediately.

Pepper's Tuna Casserole

Ingredients:

6 1/2 oz water-packed tuna

1/2 cup of onion; diced

6 oz. of egg noodles

1 can of light cream mushroom soup

Salt to taste

Pepper to taste

2 slices of light sandwich cheese

Directions:

1. First, cook the noodles and drain them.
2. Next, mix in all the listed ingredients and top with the cheese.
3. Place in the oven and bake at 350 degrees for about 45 minutes to 1 hour.
4. Serve.

Prairie Oyster

Ingredients:

1 FL oz. of brandy

1 teaspoon of catsup

1 pinch of coarse pepper

1 pinch of cayenne pepper

1/2 fl oz of Worcestershire sauce

1/2 fl oz of vinegar

1 egg yolk

Directions:

1. First, shake all the ingredients, with the exception of the egg yolk, over ice and strain into old fashioned glass over two ice cubes.
2. Next, very carefully add the yolk without breaking.
3. Gulp it down in one-shot.

Quick Fish Chowder

Ingredients:

1 tablespoon of safflower oil
1 large onion or leek
3 large potatoes; cubed
2 carrots; cut into chunks
1/4 cup of chopped parsley
½ teaspoon of dried dill
1/4 teaspoon of salt
6 cups of water
1 lb. of firm fish; cut in 1-inch pieces
1 paprika for garnish

Directions:

1. In a large pot, sauté the onions in oil until translucent.
2. Add vegetables, water, and seasonings and simmer for 20 minutes.
3. For a creamier texture, puree part of the soup and return to the pot.
4. Add fish and simmer 10 minutes more.
5. Serve in bowls and garnish with paprika.

Rainbow Trout Provencal

Ingredients:

2 tablespoons of butter
2 garlic cloves, finely chopped
1 bell pepper, julienne
1/2 medium onion, cut into strips
1 teaspoon of fennel seeds
6 tablespoons of dry vermouth or white wine
2 tablespoons of tomato paste
2 tablespoons of chopped fresh parsley
Salt and pepper
4 trout fillets (4 oz. each)

Directions:

1. First, mix the butter and garlic, bell peppers, onions and fennel seeds together in a microwavable dish.
2. Cover up the ingredients and microwave on full power for about two minutes.
3. Next, stir in the vermouth, tomato paste and parsley.
4. Season the mixture with salt and pepper.
5. Next, place the trout fillets, with the flesh-side down, on vegetable mixture. Cover up and cook for 2 minutes.
6. Rotate the dish and cook for an additional 1 to 2 minutes longer, or until fish flakes when tested with a fork.
7. Next, place the trout on serving plate and top with vegetable mixture.
8. Garnish with additional parsley.
9. Serve.

Rotini & Crab

Ingredients:

8 oz rotini -- or corkscrew
1 pack of pasta
20 oz bag frozen broccoli -or-
1 1/2 lb. of fresh broccoli
2 tablespoons of margarine – reduced calorie
1 tablespoon of olive oil
1 teaspoon of garlic -- minced
2 medium zucchini -- sliced
1/4 cup of scallions -- sliced
12 oz. of crab meat
2 oz grated parmesan cheese --divided
1/2 teaspoon of salt
1/2 teaspoon of pepper

Directions:

1. First, cook the pasta. Add the broccoli 5 minutes before the end of the cooking time.

2. Cover the pot and return to boil. Proceed to cook for additional 5 minutes.
3. Drain and rinse under cold water; set aside.

4. Heat the margarine and oil, add garlic, zucchini, scallions and crab. Cook for about 2 to 3 minutes.

5. Add the pasta and broccoli and heat through.

6. Add 1 ounce cheese, salt and pepper.

7. Garnish with the remaining ounce of cheese before serving.
8. Serve.

Sesame Salmon Steaks

Ingredients:

4 salmon steaks; 6-8 oz each

3 tablespoons of tahini

2 tablespoons of toasted chili sesame seed oil

1 cup of brown oil

2 tablespoons of white sesame seeds

1 teaspoon of ginger, powdered

1 teaspoon of cracked black pepper

Directions:

1. First, clean and dry the salmon. Whisk together all ingredients, with the exception of the salmon, in a small bowl.
2. Pour into a gallon-sized zip-seal plastic bag along with fish. Seal and refrigerate at least 8 hours.
3. Remove the salmon from the marinade and pat dry. While the grill is still hot, place the salmon on the grill and cook for around 6 to 7 minutes per side.
4. Serve.

    P. S - the steaks may also be broiled, 10 minutes per inch thickness

Seven Minute Boiled Crawfish

Ingredients:

50 lb. of crawfish, live

2 ice cream salt, boxes

4 oz liquid crab boils

3 cayenne

6 bay leaves, whole

6 celery

4 onions, medium

3 lemons or 1 tsp. of lemon oil

8 oz. of honey

3 oranges, halved

Directions:

1. Pour about 30 qt. of water in a suitably-sized pot.
2. Proceed to add all the ingredients except crawfish, apply heat and bring to a boil.
3. Next, add the crawfish. When it boils again, time for 7 minutes.
4. Remove from fire, add one bucket of cold water. Let it soak for one hour.

Shark Steaks

Ingredients:

1 lb. or more of edible shark fill (cut into 1/4 thick steaks)

1/4 cup of lime or lemon juice, or more

1 teaspoon of salt, or to taste

1/4 cup of corn oil

Directions:

1. First, marinate the shark in the lime juice and salt for at least an hour.
2. Heat the oil in a frying pan over moderate heat.
3. Next, drain the shark steaks well and fry them for a minute on either side.
4. Serve while still warm.

Shrimp Brochette

Ingredients:

1 stick of butter

2 cloves of garlic

1 lemon juice

1/2 bacon for each shrimp

Salt & pepper to taste

Directions:

1. First, apply heat to the lemon juice, butter and garlic until boiling point.
2. Position half slice of bacon around each shrimp.
3. Add salt and pepper to taste.
4. Proceed to broil for about 15-20 minutes while turning once.
5. Serve.

Simple Scallops Supreme

Ingredients:

2 lb. of scallops

4 oz of canned mushrooms

1 can (10 oz) of cream mushroom soup

1/4 cup of sherry

1/2 teaspoon of tarragon

1 bread crumbs (topping)

1 grated cheese (topping)

Directions:

1. Mix all the listed ingredients together, with the exception of the toppings. Cut the large scallops in half, and place them on individual baking shells or a shallow rectangular casserole dish.
2. Sprinkle with medium layers of bread crumbs and grated cheese.
3. Place in the oven and proceed to bake at 350 degrees for an hour.
4. Remove from the oven and serve.

So Easy Fish

Ingredients:

2 fillets of white fish, 8 oz.

1/4 cup of fresh bread crumbs

1/8 teaspoon of garlic powder

1/2 teaspoon of oil

1 teaspoon of grated parmesan cheese

1/8 teaspoon of lemon pepper

Directions:

1. Preheat your oven to a temperature of 425 degrees Fahrenheit.
2. Then, rinse the fish and pat dry.
3. Next, grease a small shallow baking pan lightly with some oil.
4. Rub the remaining oil over the top of the fish.
5. In a small bowl, mix the remaining ingredients together and sprinkle over the fish.
6. Place this in the oven and bake, while uncovered, for about 20 minutes or until the fish flakes easily.
7. Serve.

Swordfish Kebabs

Ingredients:

2 1/4 lb. of swordfish steaks
6 tablespoons of olive oil
1 teaspoon of oregano, chopped
1 teaspoon of marjoram, chopped
1 juice & rind from half a lemon
4 tomatoes, cut in thick slices
2 lemons, cut in thin slices
Salt and fresh ground pepper
Lemon slices/Italian parsley

Directions:

1. Cut the swordfish steaks into two-inch pieces.
2. Then, mix the olive oil, herbs, lemon juice and rind together and set aside for further use.
3. Next, thread the swordfish, tomato slices and lemon slices on skewers, while alternating the ingredients along the skewers.
4. Brush the skewers with the oil and lemon juice mixture and cook under a preheated broiler for about 10 minutes, basting frequently with the lemon and oil.
5. Serve garnished with lemons and parsley.

The Perfect Tuna Casserole

Ingredients:

1 can of cream of mushroom soup

1/3 cup of milk

6 1/2 oz of tuna; drained and flaked

2 eggs; hard boiled, sliced

1 cup of peas; cooked

1 cup of potato chips, slightly crumbled

Directions:

1. First, preheat the oven to a temperature of 350 degrees Fahrenheit.
2. Next, blend the soup and milk in a casserole dish.
3. Then, stir in the tuna, eggs, and peas.
4. Place the casserole dish in the oven and bake for 20 minutes.
5. Top with the slightly crumbled chips. Return to the oven and bake for another 10 minutes.
6. Remove from the oven and serve.

Tomato-Fish Cossack Stew

Ingredients:

2 onions, chopped
2 garlic cloves, minced
1 tablespoon of oil
36 tomatoes peeled or 16 oz. of canned stewed tomatoes
8 oz. of tomato sauce
1 potato
2 tablespoons of dill, freshly chopped
1 teaspoon of thyme leaves
1 tablespoon of lemon juice, fresh
3 bay leaves
1/4 teaspoon of black pepper
1 tablespoon of parsley, chopped
2 lb. of fish, boneless & cubed

Directions:

1. First, cook the onions and garlic together in oil till they are tender.

2. Next, cut up the tomatoes.

3. Peel and chop the potato.

4. Then, stir in the tomatoes, tomato sauce, potato, dill, bay leaves, thyme, and pepper.

5. Place on a heat source and bring to boil. Then, reduce the heat, cover, and simmer for 30 minutes.

6. Next, stir in the fish, lemon juice, & parsley.

7. Bring to boil and then reduce the heat. Cover and allow to simmer for an extra 3-5 minutes.

8. Serve

Trout Appétit With Remoulade Sauce

Ingredients:

1 1/2 lb. of smoked trout

Remoulade sauce Ingredients:

4 tablespoons of horseradish mustard
1/2 cup of tarragon vinegar
2 tablespoons of catsup
1 tablespoon of paprika
1/2 teaspoon of cayenne pepper
1 teaspoon of salt
1 clove of garlic
1 cup of salad oil
1/2 cup of shallots
1/2 cup of chopped celery

Directions:

1. First, peel the fish by removing the skin and bones from the fish.
2. Next, flake and place in cocktail glasses or iced supreme bowls lined with lettuce.
3. Place all the listed ingredients for Remoulade Sauce in a blender and blend together thoroughly.
4. Chill well before serving.

Tuna Apple Salad

Ingredients:

6 1/2 oz of tuna

3 cups of torn lettuce

1 apple

1 stalk of celery, chopped

4 1/4 oz of chopped olives (optional)

1/4 cup of cheese, grated (optional)

1 boiled egg, chopped (optional)

3 tablespoons of Thousand Island dressing

Directions:

1. First, wash the tuna very carefully and drain the tuna.
2. Then, tear up the lettuce leaves into small bite-sized pieces.
3. Next, proceed to core the apple and cut into eight wedges.
4. Cut up each wedge crosswise into 4 or 5 chunks. Each apple piece should still have peel on one edge. (red apples look nice for this recipe)
5. Next, mix the tuna, lettuce, apple & chopped celery.
6. Proceed to add any or all of the optional ingredients as desired.
7. Add the Thousand Island dressing and toss until well blended.
8. Serve with crackers or specialty bread.

Tuna In A Shell

Ingredients:

6 oz of tuna; drained
1/2 cup of cheddar cheese, shredded
1/2 cup of celery; finely chopped
1/4 cup of onion; finely chopped
1/4 cup of mayonnaise
2 tablespoons of pimento; chopped
1 teaspoon of chives; chopped
1 teaspoon of lemon juice
1/2 teaspoon of salt
1 dash of pepper
2 tablespoons of dry bread crumbs
2 tablespoons of butter
4 baking shells; 1/2-cup size

Directions:

1. Using a suitable container, mix the first ten listed ingredients together (starting from the tuna to the dash of pepper).
2. Next, split the mixture into the shells (alternatively, you can use small casseroles dishes).
3. Sprinkle them with all over with the bread crumbs and dot with butter.
4. Place them in the oven and bake at 350 degrees Fahrenheit for 15 minutes or until the top is lightly browned.
5. Remove from oven and serve.

Vegetable Fish Fillets

Ingredients:

1 lb. of sole or cod fillets
1 tablespoon of oil
1 cup of sliced onions
3 cup of sliced zucchini
1 cup of green pepper slices
3/4 cup of chopped tomatoes
3 tablespoons of dry sherry (optional)
1 tablespoon of lemon juice
1/2 teaspoon of salt
1/2 teaspoon of basil
1/4 teaspoon of pepper
2 drops of hot pepper sauce
1/4 cup parmesan cheese

Directions:

1. Place the filets in a layer in an oiled 9-inch square baking pan.

2. Sauté the onion, zucchini and green pepper in oil until they are crisp and tender.

3. Next, spoon this mixture over the fillets.

4. Top with tomatoes.

5. Next, mix the sherry, lemon juice, salt, basil, pepper and pepper sauce together.

6. Pour over the fillets.

7. Place in the oven and bake while uncovered at 350 degrees Fahrenheit for about 25-30 minutes.
8. Remove the fish and vegetables and place on a heated platter. Sprinkle with the parmesan cheese.

Whitefish Baked With Fiddlehead Ferns

Ingredients:

1/2 cup of white wine
2 tablespoons of Dijon mustard
4 (7-oz) of whitefish fillets
Salt and white pepper to taste
1/2 teaspoon of thyme
3/4 lb. of fiddlehead ferns or asparagus
1 medium onion; finely diced
2 tablespoons of unsalted butter

Directions:

1. Pre-heat the oven to 375 degrees Fahrenheit.

2. Then, mix the wine and mustard in a 3-inch deep baking dish that is large enough to hold the whitefish fillets in one layer.

3. Place the whitefish in the wine and sprinkle with salt, pepper and thyme.

4. Next, place the onions and fiddleheads on top and cover up the dish.

5. Transfer to the oven and bake for 20 minutes.

6. Remove the baking dish from the oven and proceed to arrange a bed of onions and fiddleheads on a platter and place the fish on top.

7. Swirl butter into the cooking liquid and pour over the fish.

8. Serve immediately.

Chunky Seafood Chowder

Ingredients
1 medium onion, chopped 2 tablespoons butter or margarine 2 pints half-and-half cream 1 (10.75 ounce) can condensed New England clam chowder, undiluted 3 medium potatoes, peeled and cubed 1 teaspoon salt 1/4 teaspoon white pepper 1 (8 ounce) package imitation crab meat, flaked

Directions
In a saucepan, saute onion in butter until tender. Add cream and canned chowder; bring to a boil. Stir in the potatoes, salt and pepper. Reduce heat; simmer, uncovered, for 15-20 minutes or until the potatoes are tender. Stir in crab and heat through.

Seafood Stuffed Mushrooms

Ingredients
2 pounds fresh mushrooms, stems removed 2 (8 ounce) packages cream cheese, softened 2 green onions, chopped 1/4 pound imitation crabmeat 1/4 pound small shrimp - peeled and deveined 2 (1 ounce) packages green onion dip mix 1 dash garlic powder salt and pepper to taste

Directions
In a medium bowl combine the cream cheese, green onions, crab, shrimp, dip mix, garlic powder, salt and pepper. Mix all together and chill mixture for about 1 hour. Spoon mixture into clean mushroom caps to stuff and serve.

Special Spicy Seafood Sauce

Ingredients

1 1/2 cups ketchup 2 tablespoons finely chopped celery 2 tablespoons white wine vinegar 2 teaspoons finely chopped green onion 2 teaspoons water 2 teaspoons Worcestershire sauce 1 teaspoon prepared horseradish 1/2 teaspoon seasoned salt 1/2 teaspoon ground mustard 1/4 teaspoon cayenne pepper

Directions
In a small bowl, combine all ingredients. Cover and refrigerate for at least 1 hour before serving. Refrigerate leftovers.

Kahala's Macaroni Seafood Salad

Ingredients
1 (16 ounce) package spaghetti, broken into 2-inch pieces 4 hard-cooked eggs, chopped 1 carrot, grated 1/2 cup frozen petite peas, thawed 1 cup frozen fully cooked salad shrimp, thawed 1/2 cup crab meat, cooked Dressing: 16 ounces mayonnaise 1/4 cup milk 1 teaspoon lemon juice 1 teaspoon sugar salt to taste black pepper to taste paprika to taste

Directions
Bring a large pot of lightly salted water to boil. Add pasta, and cook until al dente, about 8 to 10 minutes. Drain, and add pasta to a large bowl. Stir in eggs, carrots, peas, shrimp, and crab meat. Cover, and refrigerate. To make dressing, stir together mayonnaise, milk, lemon juice, and sugar. Season to taste with salt, pepper, and paprika. Mix dressing into chilled pasta, stirring until well combined. If the salad seems dry, stir in more mayonnaise and a splash more milk or water. Cover, and chill before serving.

Seafood Strata with Pesto

Ingredients

12 slices day-old sourdough bread, crusts removed 1 cup basil pesto 3 tablespoons butter 1 (10 ounce) package sliced fresh mushrooms 1 cup chopped green onion 1/4 cup dry sherry 8 ounces medium shrimp - peeled and deveined 8 ounces fresh crabmeat 2 cups shredded Swiss cheese 6 eggs 3 cups half-and-half cream 1/2 teaspoon salt 1/8 teaspoon cayenne pepper 1/2 cup panko bread crumbs 1 medium tomato, cut into wedges 1 tablespoon chopped fresh basil or chives for garnish

Directions
Preheat the oven to 350 degrees F (175 degrees C). Cut each slice of bread into 4 triangles. Place them on a baking sheet, and bake for about 10 minutes, or until toasted. Allow to cool, then spread pesto onto one side of each piece of bread. Set aside. Melt the butter in a large skillet over medium heat. Add the mushrooms; cook and stir until all of the liquid has evaporated. Add the onions; cook and stir for a couple of minutes, then pour in the sherry. Simmer for 1 minute. Place half of the bread triangles into a greased 9x13 inch baking dish with the pesto side facing up. Sprinkle half of the cheese over the bread. Spread the shrimp and crabmeat over the cheese.
Top with the mushroom and onion mixture, then sprinkle all but 1/2 cup of the remaining cheese over the mushrooms. Cover with the other half of the bread so that the pesto side is facing down. In a large bowl, whisk together the eggs, half-and-half, salt, and cayenne pepper. Pour over the entire casserole. Cover and refrigerate for at least 2 and up to 24 hours. Remove from the refrigerator for one hour before baking. Preheat the oven to 350 degrees F (175 degrees C). Combine the 1 cup of reserved cheese with the panko crumbs in a plastic bag. Shake to blend, and sprinkle over the top of the casserole. Bake uncovered for 55 to 60 minutes in the preheated oven, or until a knife inserted in the center comes out clean. Let stand for 15 minutes before serving. Garnish with fresh tomato and basil or chives.

Dipping Sauce for Seafood

Ingredients
1 1/2 cups plain non-fat yogurt 1/3 cup honey 1/2 cup prepared Dijon-style mustard 1 tablespoon chopped green onion 1 dash chili sauce

Directions
In a medium bowl, mix together plain non-fat yogurt, honey, prepared Dijon-style mustard, green onion and chili sauce. Chill in the refrigerator approximately 1 hour before serving.

Seafood And Cabbage Salad

Ingredients
2 1/2 cups shredded cabbage 1 cup shredded red cabbage 1 head fresh broccoli, cut into florets 1 green bell pepper, thinly sliced 1 red bell pepper, sliced 1 pound imitation crabmeat, coarsely chopped 3/4 cup light mayonnaise 1/4 cup lemon juice 2 tablespoons white sugar 3 tablespoons white wine vinegar 1 clove crushed garlic 1 1/2 teaspoons Worcestershire sauce 1/2 teaspoon salt 1/2 teaspoon ground black pepper 1/2 teaspoon hot pepper sauce

Directions
In a small bowl, whisk together mayonnaise, lemon juice, sugar, white wine vinegar, garlic, Worcestershire sauce, salt and pepper, and chile sauce. In a large bowl, combine cabbage, broccoli, bell peppers, and crab. Toss mixture with dressing. Cover, and refrigerate until ready to serve.

Lemon Seafood Risotto

Ingredients

2 tablespoons olive oil 1 large leek, cleaned and thinly sliced 2 cloves garlic, minced 1 cup Arborio rice 2 cups low-sodium chicken broth, divided 1 cup dry white wine 1/2 pound bay scallops 1/2 pound medium shrimp, peeled and deveined 1 cup fresh snow peas, trimmed and halved crosswise 1 medium red bell pepper, diced 3 tablespoons grated Parmesan cheese 2 teaspoons dried basil 2 tablespoons lemon juice ground black pepper to taste

Directions
Heat olive oil in a large, heavy-bottomed saucepan over medium-low heat. Cook the leek and garlic until soft, about 5 minutes. Stir in the rice, and cook for 5 minutes more, stirring frequently. Pour in 1 1/2 cups of the chicken broth, and bring to a boil over high heat, stirring occasionally. Reduce heat to medium-low, and simmer, uncovered for 5 minutes, continuing to stir. Pour in the remaining chicken broth and wine, increase heat to medium, and cook for about 5 more minutes, stirring constantly. Add the scallops, shrimp, peas, and red pepper. Cook, stirring constantly, until the remaining liquid is almost absorbed, and the seafood has cooked, about 5 minutes. When the rice is just tender and slightly creamy, season with Parmesan cheese, basil, lemon juice, and pepper.

Rachel's Crockpot Seafood Cheese Dip

Ingredients
1 (8 ounce) package processed cheese food (such as VelveetaB®) 2 tablespoons reduced-fat cream cheese 1 1/2 cups sour cream 1/2 cup cooked small shrimp 1/2 cup cooked crabmeat, flaked 1/2 cup cooked lobster, flaked 2 teaspoons seafood seasoning (such as Old BayB) 1 teaspoon Worcestershire sauce 1 loaf (1/2-inch-thick) slices French bread, lightly toaste

Directions

Combine processed cheese food, cream cheese, sour cream, shrimp, crab, and lobster in a crockpot. Cover and cook on Low heat until cheese is melted, about 1 hour, stirring occasionally to break up lumps. Once the cheese is melted, stir in seafood seasoning and Worcestershire sauce. Serve with French bread.

Seafood Pasta Delight

Ingredients
8 ounces uncooked vermicelli pasta 2 tablespoons cornstarch 1 teaspoon sugar 3/4 teaspoon salt Dash pepper 1/2 cup chicken broth 1/2 cup dry white wine or additional chicken broth 1/4 cup reduced-sodium soy sauce 1 medium sweet red pepper, julienned 1 medium sweet yellow pepper, julienned 2 cups fresh or frozen sugar snap peas 2 cloves garlic cloves, minced 1/4 teaspoon ground ginger 1 tablespoon olive or canola oil 1 pound sea scallops, halved 1 pound uncooked medium shrimp, peeled and deveined 2 teaspoons sesame oil

Directions
Cook pasta according to package directions. In a bowl, combine the cornstarch, sugar, salt and pepper; stir in the broth, wine or additional broth and soy sauce until smooth; set aside. In a large nonstick skillet or wok, stir-fry the peppers, peas, garlic and ginger in oil for 2-4 minutes or until crisp-tender. Add scallops and shrimp; stir-fry 2 minutes longer. Stir cornstarch mixture and add to the pan. Bring to a boil; cook and stir for 2 minutes or until thickened. Drain pasta; add to skillet. Heat until scallops are firm and opaque and shrimp turn pink. Sprinkle with sesame oil.

Christmas Seafood Soup

Ingredients

2 (6.5 ounce) cans chopped clams 2 cups diced peeled potatoes 2 cups chopped celery 2 cups diced carrots 1/2 cup water 2 cups milk 5 ounces frozen cooked shrimp, thawed 4 bacon strips, cooked and crumbled 2 teaspoons minced fresh parsley salt and pepper to taste

Directions
Drain the clams, reserving juice; set clam aside. In a large saucepan or Dutch oven, combine clam juice, potatoes, celery, carrots and water. Bring to a boil. Reduce heat; cover and cook for 15 minutes or until vegetables are tender. Add the milk, shrimp, bacon, parsley, salt, pepper and reserved clams; heat through.

Seafood Nachos

Ingredients
30 baked tortilla chips 1 (8 ounce) package imitation crabmeat, chopped 1/4 cup reduced-fat sour cream 1/4 cup reduced-fat mayonnaise 2 tablespoons finely chopped onion 1/4 teaspoon dill weed 1 cup shredded reduced-fat Cheddar cheese 1/4 cup sliced ripe olives 1/4 teaspoon paprika

Directions
Arrange tortilla chips in a single layer on an ungreased baking sheet. In a bowl, combine the crab, sour cream, mayonnaise, onion and dill; spoon about 1 tablespoon onto each chip. Sprinkle with cheese, olives and paprika. Bake at 350 degrees F for 6-8 minutes or until cheese is melted.

Banana Leaf Seafood

Ingredients

6 shallots, finely chopped 4 cloves garlic, peeled and crushed 2 tablespoons sambal belachan 2 teaspoons vegetable oil 1 teaspoon curry powder 1 teaspoon ground cumin 1 teaspoon fresh lime juice salt and pepper to taste 1 pound squid, cleaned and sliced into rings 1 banana leaf

Directions
In a medium, non-reactive bowl, mix shallots, garlic, sambal belachan, vegetable oil, curry powder, cumin, lime juice, salt, and pepper. Place squid in the mixture. Cover, and marinate in the refrigerator at least 2 hours. Preheat an outdoor grill for high heat, and lightly oil grate. Lightly grease the banana leaf. Wrap squid in the leaf, and place on the prepared grill. Cook 10 to 15 minutes, until leaf is slightly charred and squid is opaque.

Seafood Chowder

Ingredients
1 tablespoon vegetable oil 1 large onion, chopped 1/4 teaspoon garlic powder 1 (10.75 ounce) can Campbell'sB Condensed Cream of Celery Soup (Regular or 98 Fat Free) 1 (10.75 ounce) can Campbell'sB Condensed Cream of Potato Soup 1 1/2 (10.75 ounce) cans milk 1/4 teaspoon dried dill weed, crushed 1/2 pound medium fresh or thawed frozen shrimp, shelled and deveined 1/2 pound fresh or thawed frozen firm white fish fillet, cut into 1-inch pieces* Chopped fresh parsley

Directions
Heat oil in saucepot. Add onion and garlic powder and cook until tender. Add soups, milk and dill. Heat to a boil. Add shrimp and fish. Cook 5 minutes over low heat or until done. Garnish with parsley.

Linguine with Seafood and Sundried Tomatoes

Ingredients

1 pound linguine pasta 1/2 cup olive oil 1/2 cup butter 4 cloves garlic, minced 1 pound bay scallops 1 pound medium shrimp - peeled and deveined 1 (8 ounce) jar clam juice 1/3 cup chopped sun-dried tomatoes 1/4 cup chopped fresh parsley 2 1/2 teaspoons lemon zest 1/4 teaspoon salt 1/4 teaspoon crushed red pepper flakes

Directions

Bring a large pot of lightly salted water to a boil. Add pasta and cook for 8 to 10 minutes or until al dente; drain. In a large skillet add the olive oil and butter. Heat until butter is melted. Add the garlic and saute until tender. Add the scallops and shrimp. Cook until shrimp is pink, about 10 minutes. Add clam juice, salt and pepper. Cook for 3 minutes more. To the cooked pasta add the tomatoes, parsley and lemon zest, toss. Pour seafood mixture over the linguini, serve immediately.

Campbell's Kitchen Seafood Bisque

Ingredients

1/4 cup sweet butter 1 pound fresh OR frozen seafood (cut-up lobster, shelled shrimp, scallops, crabmeat OR imitation crabmeat) 2 (10.75 ounce) cans Campbell'sB Condensed Cream of Shrimp Soup 2 (10.75 ounce) cans Campbell'sB Condensed Cream of Potato Soup 1 cup heavy cream 4 cups half-and-half hot pepper sauce to taste Cream sherry to taste

Directions

Melt butter in large saucepan. Add your choice of seafood and cook until done. Add soups, heavy cream and half-and-half; stir until smooth. Heat through. Season with hot pepper sauce and sherry.

Seafood Tomato Alfredo

Ingredients
1 tablespoon butter 1 medium onion, chopped 1 (10.75 ounce) can Campbell's® Condensed Cream of Mushroom with Roasted Garlic Soup 1/2 cup milk 1 cup diced canned tomato 1 pound fresh fish fillet (flounder, haddock or halibut), cut into 2-inch pieces 4 cups hot cooked linguine

Directions
Heat the butter in a 10-inch skillet over medium heat. Add the onion and cook until it's tender. Stir in the soup, milk and tomatoes. Heat to a boil. Add the fish to the skillet and reduce the heat to low. Cover and cook for 10 minutes or until the fish flakes easily when tested with a fork. Serve over linguine.

A Simple Seafood Bisque

Ingredients
1 (12 ounce) can evaporated milk 1/2 cup half-and-half 1/2 cup dry white wine 1 roasted red pepper, chopped 2 teaspoons butter 1 bay leaf 1 pinch salt 1 dash hot pepper sauce (such as Tabasco) 2 (8 ounce) cans oysters, drained and rinsed 2 (6.5 ounce) cans chopped clams with juice 1 cup chopped portobello mushrooms 2 green onions, minced

Directions
Heat evaporated milk, half-and-half, white wine, roasted red pepper, butter, bay leaf, salt, and hot pepper sauce in a saucepan over medium-low heat, stirring often, until very hot but not simmering, about 5 minutes. Stir in the oysters, clams with juice, and mushrooms. Cover and cook until canned oysters

are just heated through, about 3 minutes. Do not boil. Remove bay leaf, sprinkle with green onions, and serve.

Seafood Salad Supreme

Ingredients
1 tablespoon butter 1 pound fresh shrimp, peeled and deveined 1 pound crabmeat 1 (8 ounce) package seashell pasta 2 strips celery, sliced 1 red bell pepper, chopped 1 green onion, thinly sliced 1 cup shredded mozzarella cheese 1/4 cup slivered, toasted almonds 1 cup mayonnaise 3 tablespoons fresh lemon juice 2 tablespoons chopped fresh parsley 1/2 teaspoon Old Bay Seasoning

Directions
In a large skillet, melt the butter over medium heat and saute shrimp until pink. Add crabmeat and cook one more minute or until heated through. Set aside. Bring a large pot of lightly salted water to a boil. Add pasta and cook for 8 to 10 minutes or until al dente; drain. Transfer the shrimp and crabmeat to a large mixing bowl and let cool to room temperature. Stir in pasta, celery, bell pepper and green onion. Add mozzarella cheese, slivered toasted almonds, mayonnaise and lemon juice. Season with parsley, and old bay seasoning. Toss to mix thoroughly. Refrigerate for 2 hours before serving.

Ben's Seafood Dip

Ingredients
1 (8 ounce) package cream cheese 1 (.25 ounce) package unflavored gelatin 1 (10.75 ounce) can condensed cream of mushroom soup 3/4 cup chopped celery 3/4 cup chopped green onions 3/4 cup water chestnuts, drained 1 1/2 cups cooked shrimp, peeled and deveined

Directions

Place the cream cheese and gelatin in a medium bowl and microwave on high approximately 1 minute, or until melted. Blend until creamy. Stir in the cream of mushroom soup, celery, green onions, water chestnuts and shrimp. Chill in the refrigerator approximately 1 hour before serving.

Mediterranean Seafood Salad

Ingredients
1 1/2 cups dried small pasta shells 3 cups imitation crab or lobster meat 2 stalks celery, finely chopped 3/4 cup black olives 1 1/2 cups mayonnaise 1/3 cup Catalina salad dressing 2 teaspoons Worcestershire sauce 1 tablespoon hot sauce 1/4 teaspoon Dijon mustard 1 cup cubed Cheddar cheese

Directions
Bring a large pot of lightly salted water to a boil. Add pasta, and cook until al dente, about 8 to 10 minutes. Drain, and place pasta in a large bowl. Stir in crabmeat, celery, and olives. Mix in mayonnaise, Catalina dressing, Worcestershire sauce, hot sauce, and Dijon. Stir in Cheddar cheese, cover, and chill at least 1 hour.

Chunky Seafood Sauce

Ingredients
1/2 cup ketchup 3/4 cup finely chopped celery 1/2 cup finely chopped green pepper 3 tablespoons finely chopped onion 2 tablespoons lemon juice 1/2 teaspoon prepared mustard 1/4 teaspoon salt 1/4 teaspoon paprika 1/4 teaspoon Worcestershire sauce

Directions

In a bowl, combine all ingredients. Cover and refrigerate for at least 1 hour before serving.

Seafood Lasagna I

Ingredients
1 (16 ounce) package lasagna noodles 1 pound cooked salad shrimp 1 pound fresh crab meat 3 tablespoons butter 3 tablespoons all-purpose flour 3 cups milk 1 cup grated Parmesan cheese 5 cups shredded mozzarella cheese

Directions
Cook lasagna noodles in a large pot of boiling salted water until al dente. Drain well. Preheat oven to 350 degrees F (175 degrees C). In a medium size saucepan over medium heat melt butter or margarine, stir in flour and let flour brown slightly. Stir in milk, stirring constantly until sauce thickens. Add the parmesan cheese to the sauce and stir well. In a 9x13 baking pan spread a thin layer of white sauce, followed by a layer of cooked lasagna noodles. Place 1/4 of the shrimp, 1/4 of the crabmeat and 1 cup mozzarella cheese on top of the lasagna noodles. Repeat three times, making four layers. Top the final layer with sauce and remaining mozzarella cheese. Bake for 45 minutes or until top is brown.

Cajun Seafood Pasta

Ingredients
2 cups heavy whipping cream 1 tablespoon chopped fresh basil 1 tablespoon chopped fresh thyme 2 teaspoons salt 2 teaspoons ground black pepper 1 1/2 teaspoons crushed red pepper flakes 1 teaspoon ground white pepper 1 cup chopped green onions 1 cup chopped parsley 1/2 pound shrimp, peeled and deveined

1/2 pound scallops 1/2 cup shredded Swiss cheese 1/2 cup grated Parmesan cheese 1 pound dry fettuccine pasta

Directions

Cook pasta in a large pot of boiling salted water until al dente. Meanwhile, pour cream into large skillet. Cook over medium heat, stirring constantly, until just about boiling. Reduce heat, and add herbs, salt, peppers, onions, and parsley. Simmer 7 to 8 minutes, or until thickened. Stir in seafood, cooking until shrimp is no longer transparent. Stir in cheeses, blending well. Drain pasta. Serve sauce over noodles.

Part 2

1. Baked Mussels And Cockles

Serves 4

Ingredients:

- 1 lb wild caught mussels, cleaned
- 1 lb wild caught cockles, cleaned
- 1 large red onion, finely chopped
- 2 lemons, juiced and zested
- Large handful of parsley
- Large handful of fresh thyme
- 2 Tbsp of coconut oil, melted

Vinaigrette Ingredients:

- 2 Tbsp red wine vinegar
- 1 Tbsp mustard of choice
- 1 large red onion, finely chopped
- Sea salt and ground pepper to taste
- 2 Tbsp extra virgin olive oil

Instructions:

1) Preheat oven 450F.

2) Clean the mussels and cockles – remove the beard and soak for 20 minutes to clean.

3) Place mussels, cockles, lemon zest, lemon juice, herbs, coconut oil, sea salt and pepper in the center of aluminum foil and seal up.

4) Bake for 10 minutes. Prepare the vinaigrette. In a bowl, mix mustard, olive oil, vinegar, sea salt and pepper.

5) When mussels and cockles are ready, serve immediately – pour in a bowl and drizzle with vinaigrette.

2. Garlic-Butter Cockles

Serves 4

Ingredients:

- 3 lbs wild caught cockles
- 3 cloves garlic, finely chopped
- Juice of 1 lemon
- 1 tsp smoked paprika
- 2 Tbsp raw grass fed butter
- 2 Tbsp sea salt + sea salt for seasoning

Instructions:

1) In a saucepan on medium-low heat, add garlic and butter together and sauté for 1 minute or until aromatic.

2) Add lemon juice and spices and season to taste with sea salt and freshly ground black pepper.

3) Bring a pot of water to the boil in a large pan over high heat and add the 2 Tbsp of sea salt and cockles; cover and cook for 2 minutes or until cockles open.

4) Drain in a colander and divide among bowls.

5) Top with garlic-butter sauce.

3. Crab Cakes

Serves 4

Ingredients:

- 1 lb wild caught crab meat
- 1 green onion, minced
- 3 Tbsp Paleo mayo
- 1 Tbsp lemon juice
- 1 pasture raised egg
- 1/3 cup nutritional yeast
- 1 garlic clove, minced
- 1/2 tsp Dijon mustard
- 1/4 cup celery, minced
- Sea salt and ground pepper to taste
- 1-2 tsp of coconut oil

Instructions:

1) Combine all ingredients. Take a 1/3 measuring cup and fill it with the mixture. Turn it out into your hand and smash it into a flat, round disk, about 1/4" thick. Do this until you run out of the mixture.

2) Heat coconut oil over medium-low heat. Once hot, add the crab cakes.

3) Cook on each side for about 7-8 minutes on each side. Be very careful when flipping. Cook until they brown then plate.

4. Herb Steamed Cockles

Serves 4

Ingredients:

- 2 1/2 lbs wild caught cockles, scrubbed and rinsed
- 2 Tbsp chopped parsley
- 1 large shallot, minced
- 1/2 cup organic dry white wine
- 1 tsp of coconut oil

Instructions:

1) In a large pot, heat the oil on medium-low. Add the shallot and cook until translucent, about 3-5 minutes. Then add wine and cover for 5 minutes until cockles open.

2) Stir the parsley into the cockles and transfer to the bowls.

5. Crab Cakes With Lemon Aioli

Serves 3-4

Crab Cake Ingredients:

- 1 lb wild caught crab meat
- 1 green onion
- 3 Tbsp Paleo Mayo (Recipe is in the Condiments book)
- 1 Tbsp lemon juice
- 1 pasture raised egg
- 1/3 cup nutritional yeast
- 1 garlic clove
- 1/2 tsp Dijon mustard
- 1/4 cup celery, minced
- Sea salt and ground pepper to taste
- 1-2 tsp of coconut oil

Lemon Aioli Ingredients:

- 6 oz plain Greek yogurt, full fat
- 3 garlic cloves, minced
- 1/4 cup parsley, chopped
- 1 lemon, juiced
- 1 tsp smoked paprika
- Sea salt and ground pepper to taste

Instructions:

1) Prepare the crab cakes mixture and form into the patties or cakes.

2) Place in fridge for about 30 minutes. This process will help make the crab cakes stick together better for forming and cooking.

3) Start forming crab cakes by spooning about 1/3 cup into your hand. Squeeze to remove any excess moisture. Roll into a ball then flatten to make it look like a disk.

4) Heat the coconut oil in a large frying pan over medium-low heat.

5) Once the coconut oil is completely melted and up to temperature, begin frying the crab cakes.

6) Cook on each side for about 7-8 minutes on each side. Be very careful when flipping.

7) Place on a serving dish and top with a drizzle of the lemon aioli.

6. Crab Cakes Benedict

Serves 3-4

Crab Cake Ingredients:

- 1 lb wild caught crab meat
- 1 green onion
- 3 Tbsp Paleo Mayonnaise (Recipe is in the Condiments book)
- 1 Tbsp lemon juice
- 1 pasture raised egg
- 1/3 cup nutritional yeast
- 1 garlic clove
- 1/2 tsp Dijon mustard
- 1/4 cup celery, minced
- Sea salt and ground pepper to taste
- 1-2 tsp of coconut oil

Hollandaise Ingredients:

- 2 Tbsp clarified butter or ghee, melted
- 3 large pasture raised egg yolks
- 2 Tbsp lemon juice, freshly squeezed
- 1 Tbsp cold filtered water
- Sea salt to taste
- Pinch of smoked paprika

Instructions:

1) Prepare the crab cakes mixture and form into the patties or cakes.

2) Bring two inches of water to a simmer in the bottom half of a double boiler.

3) Start making the Hollandaise by whisking the eggs with the cold water in the top half until light and foamy. Add a few drops of lemon juice and continue whisking over the simmering water until the egg yolks have begun to thicken.

4) Begin whisking 1 Tbsp of clarified butter into the egg yolks slowly – just a bit at a time. Incorporate all the egg yolks until the sauce is smooth and thickened then add the remaining lemon juice. Season with sea salt.

5) Melt 1 Tbsp of ghee in a large sauté pan or skillet over medium-low heat. Crack the 3 eggs carefully into the pan and cook until the egg whites have set. With a large, thin, flexible spatula carefully flip the eggs, taking care not to break the yolks. Immediately remove from the heat and set aside.

7. Crab And Asparagus Frittata

Serves 4

Ingredients:
- 1 cup asparagus, chopped
- 1/4 pound of wild caught crab meat
- 8 pasture raised eggs
- 1 cup mushrooms, chopped
- 1/2 cup green onions
- 1/2 cup bell pepper
- 1/4 cup filtered water
- 1/4 dried oregano
- 1/4 dried thyme
- 1/4 dried rosemary
- Sea salt and ground pepper to taste
- 1-2 tsp of coconut oil

Instructions:

1) Preheat oven to 375F. Grease a 10-inch nonstick skillet with coconut oil and heat over medium-low heat.

2) Add the asparagus, mushrooms, onions and bell pepper; sauté until crisp-tender, about 7-8 minutes the remove and add a crab meat then mix well.

3) In a separate bowl whisk eggs, water, rosemary, thyme and oregano in medium bowl until blended. Pour over crab mixture

in skillet. Cook over medium-low heat until eggs are set at edges, 7-8 minutes.

4) Place into the oven and bake for 8-10 minutes or until browned.

8. Avocado King Crab Shooters

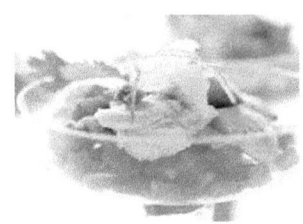

Serves 4

Ingredients:
- 2 small Hass avocados, cut into 8 wedges
- 1/2 lb wild caught king crab
- 3 Tbsp coconut milk, full fat
- 1 Tbsp fresh lemon juice
- 1 Tbsp fresh ginger, grated
- Sea salt and ground pepper to taste

Instructions:

1) In a shallow bowl, coarsely mash the diced avocado with a fork. Add the lemon juice and mash the mixture just until combined. Stir in the chopped parsley and season generously with sea salt and pepper.

2) With kitchen scissors, cut the crab leg shells and pull out the crab meat. Add pieces into a small bowl, combine the coconut milk and ginger. Fold in the crab and season with sea salt and pepper.

3) Spoon the crab and avocado into 8 small glasses. Top each shooter with an avocado wedge and serve.

9. Grilled Snow Crab Legs

Serves 6-8

Ingredients:
- 4 lbs wild caught snow crab legs
- 6 garlic cloves, minced
- 5-6 Tbsp raw grass fed butter
- 2 Tbsp coconut oil, melted
- Sea salt to taste

Instructions:

1) Preheat grill to high heat. When hot, lightly oil grate.

2) Whisk together the coconut oil, butter, and garlic; generously brush onto crab. Top with sea salt to taste.

3) Cook crab on preheated grill, turning once, until the shell begins to brown, about 6-7 minutes.

10. Spicy Crab Stuffed Cucumber Cups

Serves 4

Ingredients:

- 3/4 cup wild caught crab meat, excess water removed
- 2 English cucumbers
- 1/4 cup Paleo sour cream (Recipe is in the Condiments book)
- 1/2 Jalapeño, seeded and minced
- 1 tsp brown mustard
- Sea salt and pepper to taste

Instructions:

1) Remove the peel from the cucumbers using a vegetable peeler. Cut the cucumber into 2 inch slices. Using a small melon baller, or spoon, scoop out most of the inside. Leave the walls and a thick portion of the bottom intact to create the cup.

2) In a bowl, combine the sour cream and add the remaining ingredients; stir until combined. Fill each of the cucumber cups with the crab dip and refrigerate until ready to serve.

11. Crab Stuffed Mushrooms

Yields 6

Ingredients:

- 6 medium sized Portobello mushrooms about 2" in diameter
- 1/2 lb wild caught crab meat
- 1 pasture raised egg
- 1 Tbsp chives, chopped
- 2 Tbsp of Paleo mayo (Recipe is in the Condiments book)
- 1/4 cup nutritional yeast
- 1 Tbsp Old Bay seasoning
- 1 tsp mustard
- Sea salt and ground pepper to taste

Instructions:

1) Preheat oven to 375F.

2) In a bowl combine crab meat, chives, egg, mustard, Paleo mayo, and Old Bay. Add nutritional yeast to bind.

3) Take the stems off the mushrooms and spoon on about 1 Tbsp of the crab filling into the center of the mushroom caps.

4) Bake for 20-25 minutes or until the filling is golden.

12. Grilled Crab In A Garlic-Herb-Butter

Serves 2

Ingredients:

1 lb wild caught snow crabs
- 1 garlic clove, minced
- 1 Tbsp parsley, minced
- 3 Tbsp raw grass fed butter
- Sea salt and ground pepper to taste

Instructions:

1) Cut a slit, length-wise, into the shell of each piece of crab.
2) Melt the butter in a large skillet over medium-low heat. Add and cook the garlic in the butter for 1 minute or until fragrant; stir in the parsley, sea salt, and pepper.
3) Add the crab legs; toss to coat; allow to simmer in the butter mixture until completely heated, 7-8 minutes.

13. Sichuan Crawfish

Serves 4

Ingredients:

- 2 lbs wild caught crawfish
- 10 whole garlic cloves
- 5 slices fresh ginger
- 8 dried red chilies
- Bundle of cilantro, chopped
- 1 Tbsp raw honey
- 1 coconut oil
- 1/2 cup filtered water
- Sea salt to taste

Instructions:

1) Soak the live crawfish in cold water with some sea salt for half an hour. Rinse them a under cold water.

2) Heat up a wok or deep sauté pan with the coconut oil on medium-low. Add in garlic cloves, ginger and dried chilis, cook until garlic becomes aromatic (1-2 minutes).

3) Toss in the crawfish and stir continuously for 1-2 minutes.

4) Add in all the seasonings, water, cilantro and cover the wok or pan for 5-7 minutes.

14. Steamed King Crab Legs

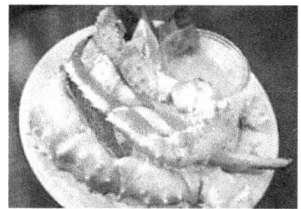

Serves 4

Ingredients:

- 2 1/2 lbs cooked and chilled wild caught King crab legs and claws, cracked and legs cut in half crosswise
- 3 cups fish stock
- 4 garlic cloves, minced
- Sea salt and ground pepper to taste
- 1/4 cup raw grass fed butter, or Ghee

Instructions:

1) Melt butter in a large skillet over mediumlow heat. Add garlic and cook 1 minute or until aromatic. Add stock, sea salt, pepper and crab legs. Cover and simmer 7-8 minutes.

2) Cook in batches until all the crab is mixed.

15. Steamed Thai Clams

Serves 2

Ingredients:

- 12 oz wild caught clams, rinsed and scrubbed
- 1 stalk lemongrass, chopped
- 3 dried chilis
- 1/2 cup coconut water
- 1 lime, juiced
- 4 kaffir lime leaves, bruised slightly
- 1 tsp coconut oil
- Sea salt to taste

Instructions:

1) Heat up a wok with the oil on medium-low. When the oil is heated, add the lemongrass, dried chilis and stir.

2) Add the clams and stir to combine. Next add the coconut water.

3) Add the kaffir lime leaves and cover the wok. Cook the clams for about 2-3 minutes or until all clams are open.

4) Add salt and lime juice. Stir to mix then serve in bowls.

16. Stuffed "Poo Cha" Crab

Serves 2-4

Ingredients:

- 6-8 wild caught blue shell crabs
- 8 oz pasture raised ground pork
- 4 oz wild caught crab meat
- 2 oz wild caught shrimp, peeled and minced
- 3 shallots, minced
- 3 pasture raised eggs
- 4 coriander leaves, finely chopped
- 1 tsp coconut oil
- Sea salt and ground pepper to taste

Instructions:

1) In a bowl, mix the pork, crab meat, shrimp, shallots, 1 egg, coriander, salt and pepper for the filling and blend well.

2) Stuff the filling into the empty crab shells using a spoon. Smooth out the surface with the back of the spoon. Steam the stuffed crab in a pot of 1" water (covered) for 5 minutes then remove.

3) Cool the stuffed crab to room temperature after steaming. Heat up a wok with some coconut oil.

4) Beat the two remaining eggs well. When the oil is heated, coat each crab mixture with the beaten eggs.

5) Make sure the filling is well coated with the beaten eggs. Transfer the stuffed crabs into the wok and fry them. As soon as the surface turns light to golden brown, dish out and serve immediately.

17. Garlic-Butter-Herb Crawfish Tails

Serves 4

Ingredients:

- 2 lb peeled wild caught crawfish tails
- 2 tsp garlic, minced
- 1/3 cup raw grass fed butter
- 2 cups chopped onions
- 1 cup chopped celery
- 1 Tbsp coconut flour
- 3 Tbsp of fresh parsley, chopped
- 1 cup filtered water
- Sea salt and ground pepper to taste

Instructions:

1) In a large sauté pan over medium-low heat, melt the butter.

2) Add the onions, celery and sauté until the vegetables are wilted, about 10 minutes.

3) Add the crawfish and garlic to the mixture.

4) Cook the crawfish for 10 minutes, stirring occasionally. Dissolve the flour in the water then add to the crawfish mixture.

5) Season with sea salt and pepper. Stir until the mixture thickens, about 4 minutes.

6) Mix in the parsley and continue cooking a few more minutes then plate.

18. Southern Boiled Crawfish

Serves 6-8

Ingredients:

- 12 lbs live wild caught crawfish
- 2 large onions, peeled and quartered
- 3 large bell peppers, cut into cubes
- 10 whole garlic cloves
- 1 lb okra, chopped into cubes
- 1/4 cup fresh parsley, chopped
- 1/2 cup Old Bay Seasoning
- Sea salt and ground pepper to taste

Instructions:

1) Pour live crawfish into a washtub or ice chest; cover with water and then drain. Repeat 3 to 4 times until crawfish are clean. Discard any broken crawfish.

2) Mix 8 quarts water, Old Bay Seasoning, onion and garlic in large (20-quart) stockpot. Bring to boil on high heat; boil 5 minutes. Add bell peppers and okra and boil 5-7 minutes. Add crawfish and return to boil. Cover and cook 2-3 minutes.

3) Turn off heat, add parsley, salt and pepper. Let stand 20 minutes. Drain and serve.

19. French Langoustine (Large Prawns)

Serves 2-4

Ingredients:

- 8 wild caught langoustine "or large prawn" tails, peeled and deveined
- 1 leek, chopped
- 2 garlic cloves, minced
- 1/4 tsp onion powder
- 4 sprigs thyme, chopped
- 2 Tbsp raw grass fed butter
- Sea salt and ground pepper to taste
- 1 tsp coconut oil

Instructions:

1) Season the langoustine tails with sea salt and pepper. Sear in a non-stick pan over medium-low heat with coconut oil about 2 minutes then remove and set aside.

2) Add the rest of the Ingredients: except the butter to the same pan. Cook on medium-low for 5-7 minutes until leeks are cooked through.

3) Add the prawns back in and add the butter until it melts. Mix well and then serve.

20. Lemon-Butter Lobster Tails

Serves 4

Ingredients:

- Four separate - 6oz wild caught lobster tails
- 2 lemons
- 4 Tbsp raw grass fed butter
- Sea salt and ground pepper to taste

Instructions:

1) Bring grill to medium heat and thaw out lobsters if they are frozen.

2) Run a metal skewer through the tails (toward the red shell side) for support, to prevent them from curling. Get one large stockpot of water to full boil, then turn it down to a gentle boil. Plunge lobster tails into water and gently boil them for about 2 minutes then remove.

3) Place them on a cutting board, shell side (red-side) down, and slice lengthwise through the softer (whiter) shell, lengthwise.

4) Place butter inside, salt, pepper, and squeeze lemon juice directly in the shells. Place on the grill red side down and cover grill to cook 2-3 minutes.

21. Thai Steamed Mussels

Serves 2

Ingredients:

- 2 lbs wild caught mussels, cleaned & debearded
- 2 Tbsp raw grass fed butter
- 1 large shallot, minced
- 4 medium garlic cloves, minced
- 1 bay leaf
- Cilantro, chopped
- Basil, chopped
- Mint, chopped
- 1 cup filtered water
- Sea salt and ground pepper to taste

Instructions:

1) In a dutch oven on medium-low place the shallots, bay leaf and garlic until you smell the aroma (about 1-2 minutes) then add the water. Bring to a simmer.

2) Put the mussels in the dutch oven and cover for 3-5 minutes to steam.

3) Add all the herbs and the butter until the butter is all melted. Mix well and then serve.

22. Broiled Bacon Wrapped Oysters

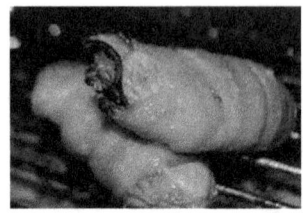

Serves 2-4

Ingredients:

- 12 wild caught oysters, shucked and rinsed
- 12 bacon slices, no nitrates or nitrites

Instructions:

1) Turn your broiler up to high and put the oven rack on the second from the top.

2) Take an oyster and wrap it around with bacon and hold together with a toothpick.

3) Place in the center of your broiler on low and place directly under the flame.

4) Cook until the bacon browns to your liking (about 5-6 minutes per side).

23. Crayfish And Spaghetti Squash Tagliatelle

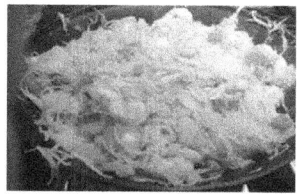

Serves 4

Ingredients:

- 1 1/2 lbs wild caught crayfish
- 1 spaghetti squash
- 1 can refrigerated coconut milk, full fat
- 1 garlic clove, minced
- 1 lemon, juiced and zested
- 2 Tbsp fresh dill, chopped
- Sea salt and ground pepper to taste
- 1 tsp coconut oil

Instructions:

1) Preheat oven to 350F. Puncture several holes throughout the spaghetti squash to allow the steam to escape. Place the spaghetti squash on a baking dish and put in the oven for 1 hour. Remove, let cool and begin to scrape with a fork to create pasta like strands. Place in a bowl.

2) Meanwhile, heat the oil in a large frying pan on medium-low. Add the garlic cook for 1 minute, or until it becomes fragrant. Add the crayfish and cook for 2-3 minutes.

3) Add spaghetti squash to pan. Scoop out the top layer of the refrigerated coconut milk which will be cream. Also add lemon zest and juice, and dill. Warm through, stir and serve.

24. Garlic Butter Mussels

Serves 2

Ingredients:

- 2 lbs wild caught mussels
- 6 cloves garlic, minced
- 2 Tbsp raw grass fed butter
- 1 cup filtered water
- Sea salt and ground pepper to taste

Instructions:

1) Place mussels in a deep pot and add 1 cup of water. Bring it to a boil and cook for 5 minutes or until all shells open up.

2) Remove mussels from pot then let it cool.

3) Separate mussels from their shells then set them aside.

4) Place a pan in medium-low heat then add butter. Once melted add garlic and mussels and sauté for 1 minute then serve.

25. Charbroiled Oysters

Serves 2-4

Ingredients:

- 12 wild caught oysters, rinsed and scrubbed
- 4 Tbsp raw grass fed butter
- 2 garlic cloves, minced
- Pinch of cayenne
- 1 Tbsp lemon juice
- 1 lemon, cut into wedges for drizzling
- 2 Tbsp Nutritional yeast
- Sea salt and ground pepper to taste

Instructions:

1) Rinse your oysters, then use a shucking knife to pry them open. Set aside the shells that are flat and will balance well on the grill.

2) While the grill is heating up, mix together all other ingredients besides the oysters and lemon juice to make the sauce/topping.

3) Set the shells on the grill and spoon a bit of topping on oysters. Let cook until just bubbling and the edges begin to curl, then fill the shells the rest of the way with any extra sauce.

4) When the sauce starts to bubble, sprinkle nutritional yeast on top and let cook until the sauce is brown on the edges of the shells.

5) Remove the oyster-filled shells from the grill and serve sizzling hot, with fresh lemon juice squeezed over the top.

26. Pico de Gallo Grilled Oysters

Serves 4

Ingredients:

- 24 wild caught oysters, rinsed and scrubbed
- 1 shallot, minced
- 2 vine-ripe tomatoes, seeded and chopped
- 2 limes
- 1/2 Jalapeño, seeded and minced
- Handful of cilantro, chopped
- Sea salt and ground pepper to taste

Instructions:

1) To make the pico de Gallo, stir the chopped tomatoes, shallot, jalapeño, cilantro together in a bowl with the juice of 1 lime and a pinch of sea salt and pepper.

2) Slice the remaining lime into thin wedges for serving.

3) Heat grill to high heat and place closed oysters on the grill and cook covered, 5-7 minutes or until opened. Remove and let cool.

4) Next use a dull knife to pry the shells completely open and discard the top shell.

5) Top with a spoonful of pico and serve immediately, with extra lime wedges.

27. Oysters Rockefeller

Serves 4

Ingredients:

- 2 dozen wild caught oysters, on the half shell
- 2 cups fresh organic spinach, chopped
- 2 shallots, minced
- 2 garlic cloves, minced
- 1 lemon, cut into wedges
- 1/2 cup nutritional yeast
- 2 Tbsp raw grass fed butter
- 3 Tbsp filtered water
- Sea salt and ground pepper to taste

Instructions:

1) Preheat the oven to 450F.

2) Melt the butter in a skillet on medium-low heat and add garlic and shallots for 1 minute.

3) Add the spinach to the pan until it wilts, approximately 3-4 minutes.

4) Add 3 Tbsp of water to help deglaze the pan. Scrape all the bits off the bottom of the pan and allow the water to reduce. Add sea salt and ground pepper to taste.

5) Spoon a bit of the spinach mixture on to each oyster, then a spoonful of nutritional yeast on top.

6) Bake for 12 minutes or until golden brown.

7) Serve with lemon wedges.

28. Half Shelled Oysters With Cucumber Mignonette

Serves 4

Ingredients:

- 24 wild caught oysters
- Lemon wedges to serve

Mignonette Ingredients:

- 1/2 English cucumber, peeled and minced
- 1/4 cup raw apple cider vinegar
- 1 shallot, minced
- 1" inch of ginger, peeled and grated
- Handful of cilantro leaves, chopped
- Sea salt and ground pepper to taste

Instructions:

1) Combine the mignonette ingredients with a fork. Cover and place in the refrigerator for at least 1 hour.

2) Clean and ready the oysters on the half shell.

3) Place on a platter with lemon wedges and the cucumber mignonette on the side to dip.

29. Baked Oysters

Serves 1-2

Ingredients:

- 4 big shell-on wild caught oysters
- 3 cloves garlic, finely chopped
- 2 Tbsp raw grass fed butter
- Parsley, chopped
- 4 lemon wedges
- Sea salt and ground pepper to taste

Instructions:

1) Shuck the oysters and set aside. Heat the oven to 375F.

2) Top the oysters with the chopped garlic, parsley leaves, and season with sea salt and ground pepper. Top with some melted butter in each oyster.

3) Bake the oysters in the oven for 20 minutes. Transfer out and serve immediately with lemon wedges.

30. Lemon-Squeezed Seared Sea Scallops

Serves 4

Ingredients:

- 1 1/2 lbs of wild caught sea scallops
- 1 lemon, juiced
- 1 Tbsp chives, minced
- 1 shallot, minced
- Sea salt and ground pepper to taste
- 1 tsp coconut oil

Instructions:

1) Heat oil in a large cast-iron skillet over medium-low heat.

2) In a bowl add all the ingredients and coat the scallops well.

3) Place scallops in the heated pan and let cook on 1 side until it turns white (approximately 3-4 minutes) then flip until done.

Onion Bombs

Ingredients
- 1/2 clove of garlic finely chopped (or use minced garlic, about a teaspoon)
- 3/4 cup of Ketchup
- 1/2 cup of crushed saltine crackers
- 1 slice of bread torn into small pieces
- Salt and pepper to taste
- 3/4 cup of shredded cheese (any kind of cheese you like)
- 1/3 cup of parmesan cheese
- optional – meatloaf seasoning packet or any extra spices or herbs that you like

Directions
- Mix all of this up with your hands as you would with meatloaf. You want about the same texture as you would with meatloaf as well. If it seems too dry, add a bit more ketchup or a splash of milk. If it feels too wet, add a little more crushed crackers.
- Now it's time to assemble your onion bombs. Start with the largest pair of onion halves. Make a large meatball and place it in one side of the onion half and place the other onion half over the top.
- Basically squishing the meatball between the 2 onion halves. Continue to fill the rest of the onion halves up with the meat mixture.
- Wrap each onion bomb in aluminum foil. You want to have enough room so that you can leave a little twist at the top so you can easily pick them up off the grill because they're hot! Now it's time to grill them.
- Slap these babies on the grill and cook for about 8-10 minutes. Flip them over on their opposite side and cook an

additional 8-10 minutes. NOTE: Grilling times will vary based on how high you have your grill set.

Crispy Bacon Grilled Cheese Roll Ups

Ingredients
- 8 slices of bread, crusts removed
- 8 slices of cheese or 1 cup+ grated cheddar
- 8 slices precooked bacon
- ¼ cup butter

Directions
- Using a rolling pin, roll slices of bread flat.
- Place one slice of cheese. Roll up bread & cheese. Wrap one slice of bacon around each roll securing with a toothpick.
- Place in a pan over medium- low heat. Add a small spoonful of butter & using tongs, rub the rolls in the butter ensuring the bread edges are covered. Continue adding bits of butter and turning with tongs until all sides are browned and cheese is melted.

Greek Grilled Chicken

Ingredients
- 6-8 boneless, skinless chicken breasts

Marinade:
- 1/2 cup extra virgin olive oil
- 1/3 cup fresh-squeezed lemon juice
- 1 tsp. fresh lemon zest or 1/4 tsp. dried lemon zest
  o 1 tsp. Greek seasoning
  o 1 tsp. poultry seasoning
  o 1 tsp. dried oregano
  o black pepper to taste

Directions

- Trim all visible fat and membranes from chicken breasts. Put chicken in single layer in Ziploc bag.
- Combine marinade ingredients and pour over chicken. Marinate in refrigerator 6-8 hours or all day if desired.
- Preheat grill to medium-hot and grill chicken 20-25 minutes, or until well browned and firm but not hard to the touch.

Grilled Zucchini Pizza Slices

Ingredients
- large zucchini slices, cut 3/4 inch thick (see recipe notes)
- Olive oil
- pizza sauce
- grated cheese
- pizza toppings of your choice

Directions
- Oil the grill grates
- Cut zucchini into thick slices about 3/4 inch thick.
- Grill the zucchini 7-8 minutes, or until there are some grill marks and it's starting to be tender.
- Remove zucchini from the grill, putting them grilled-side up on a cutting board you can use to take them to the kitchen. Add sauce, cheese, and other toppings as desired.
- Put loaded zucchini slices back on the grill and cook 7-8 minutes more with the grill lid closed.
- Remove zucchini pizzas from grill and serve hot.

Grilled Pork Chops & Sweet Potato Wedges

Ingredients

Sweet Potato Wedges Ingredients
- 2 raw sweet potatoes, cut into wedges
- 1 tablespoon olive oil
- 1/2 tsp paprika
- 1/2 tsp cinnamon
- Sea salt & pepper

Pork Chop Ingredients
- 4 bone-in pork chops
- 2 tsp paprika
- Sea salt & pepper

Honey Mustard Sauce Ingredients
- 5 tablespoons raw honey
- 2 tablespoons Dijon mustard
- 1 tablespoon apple cider vinegar

Directions
- First combine the honey mustard ingredients, then divide it into two small bowls and set aside
- Next mix the dry potato seasonings together in a small bowl
- Slice potatoes and place wedges in a medium bowl. Sprinkle potato seasonings over, coat with olive oil, then toss together
- Pre-heat grill to medium
- Season both sides of chops with paprika, salt and pepper
- Place potato wedges on grill, turning often until tender (about 10-15 minutes, depending on thickness)
- While the potato wedges are grilling, place pork chops on grill and baste with one of the containers you set aside of the honey-mustard sauce. Turn and baste chops until cooked through (usually about 5-7 minutes per side)

- Serve chops brushed with extra honey-mustard sauce from the unused container, and add the potato wedges
- Garnish with chopped green onions if desired

Grilled Vegetable Stack with Lemon Hummus

Ingredients
- 1 large red or purple onion, peeled, trimmed, sliced into 6 slices
- 2 large red bell peppers, cored, sliced into 3 pieces
- 2 large yellow bell peppers, cored, sliced into 3 pieces
- 1 large zucchini, halved, sliced lengthwise, to make 6 pieces
- 1 large yellow squash, halved, sliced lengthwise, to make 6 pieces
- 1 medium-large eggplant, trimmed, sliced into 6 pieces
- 6 large Portobello mushroom caps, stemmed, gills removed
- 1/2 cup olive oil
- 3 tablespoons balsamic vinegar
- 3 cloves fresh garlic, chopped
- 1 teaspoon each: dried thyme, dill, parsley
- Sea salt and ground pepper, to taste

Directions
- In a large bowl combine the onion, bell peppers, zucchini, yellow squash, eggplant, portabella mushrooms.
- In a glass cup combine the olive oil, balsamic vinegar, garlic, thyme, dill and parsley. Pour the marinade over the

vegetables. Season with sea salt and ground pepper, to taste. Gently toss to coat.
- Cover and marinate for one hour.
- Heat the grill to medium-high heat.
- Place the veggies in a grill basket (or spread out the veggies on a large sheet of foil). Place on the hot grill, cover and cook until the vegetables are tender crisp, about 20-25 minutes, depending upon the size of your grill.
- Remove the veggie basket/foil with vegetables to a large platter and set aside.
- To serve, create a vegetable stack. Place the Portobello mushroom cap on a serving plate and layer it with a spoonful of lemon hummus. Add the eggplant, peppers, zucchini and onion. Top with a dab of more hummus, if desired. Sprinkle with fresh chopped chives. Repeat for the remaining five servings.

Grilled Soy & Honey Mustard Vegetables

Ingredients
- 8 wooden skewers, soaked in water to prevent burning
- 1 recipe honey mustard
- 1/4 cup soy sauce
- 2 cloves garlic, smashed, peeled, and minced
- 1 teaspoon fresh-ground black pepper
- 2 bell peppers, cored, seeded, and sliced
- 2 zucchini, washed and cut into 1 inch slices
- 1 pint crimini mushrooms, brushed clean and stems removed
- 1 red onion, cut into wedges

Directions
- In a large bowl, whisk together the honey mustard, soy sauce, garlic, and black pepper. Fold the prepared vegetables into the marinade and set aside for 30 minutes. Give the vegetables a gentle stir every 10 minutes or so.
- Meanwhile, start your coals or heat up your grill pan.
- When you're ready to cook, alternate the vegetables on the prepared wooden skewers. Set on the grill and cook for about 3 minutes on each side, or until the edges are crisp and the veggies are tender.
- Remove to a plate and serve on skewers or over a bed of whole grain.

Grilled Vegetables with Chickpeas and Creamy Polenta

Ingredients
- Polenta
- 2 cups water
- 2 cups vegetable broth
- ¼ teaspoon sea salt
- 1 cup polenta
- 2 tablespoons butter

Vegetables
- 1 medium zucchini
- 1 red pepper
- 1 tablespoon olive oil or melted coconut oil
- 2 to 3 teaspoons curry powder
- ½ cup cooked chickpeas, drained and rinsed
- Feta and cilantro, garnish

Directions
- Bring the water, broth and salt to a boil. Stir in polenta; cook until polenta begins to thicken. Cover and reduce heat to lowest setting. Simmer polenta for 25 to 30 minutes, stirring and scraping the pan bottom and sides every 8 to 10 minutes. Remove from heat and stir in butter.
- Preheat grill. Slice the zucchini and pepper into strips; toss with oil and curry powder. Grill until zucchini and peppers are slightly charred, 3 to 5 minutes per side.
- Roughly chop the vegetables and toss them with the chickpeas. Divide polenta among individual serving bowls. Top with grilled vegetables, cilantro and feta.

Easy Grilled Vegetables

Ingredients
- 1 pound tomatoes, cut into large dice (if using cherry or grape tomatoes, leave whole)
- 1 yellow or white onion, peeled and ends removed, cut into eighths
- 1 medium zucchini, ends removed, sliced in half lengthwise, then cut into 1/2" pieces
- 1 medium yellow squash, ends removed, sliced in half lengthwise, then cut into 1/2" pieces
- 1 carton (8 oz.) mushrooms, cleaned and halved
- 1 bulb garlic
- 4 Tbsp. plus 1 tsp. olive oil, divided
- 3 Tbsp. balsamic vinegar
- 1 Tbsp. mixed fresh herbs (such as basil, oregano, parsley, rosemary, and/or thyme), minced (optional)
- black pepper and sea salt, freshly ground

Directions
- Prepare/set your grill to medium-high heat.
- Begin by preparing the garlic for roasting. Peel off the outer papery covering of the head of garlic.
- Using a sharp knife, slice off 1/4-inch of the top of the bulb, so that the inside of each clove is exposed.
- Place the head on a square of aluminum foil. Drizzle 1 tsp. olive oil over the top of the cloves, and then use your fingers to spread it around well.
- Fold up the foil over the top of the clove, so that it is fully enclosed. Set the foil package directly on top of the grill grates and cook, covered, for about 20 minutes (or until garlic cloves are soft and lightly golden).

- In a large bowl, combine tomatoes, onion, zucchini, squash, and mushrooms with 2 Tbsp. of olive oil and a generous amount of freshly-ground salt and pepper.
- Toss until vegetables are evenly coated. Transfer vegetables to a grill pan, and set on the grill grates (next to the foil-wrapped garlic).
- Grill, stirring every 2-3 minutes, until vegetables are tender and lightly charred. Remove garlic and vegetables from grill when cooked.
- While vegetables are cooking, prepare the dressing. In a small bowl, whisk together the remaining 2 Tbsp. of olive oil, balsamic vinegar, all of the roasted garlic cloves, and the chopped fresh herbs (optional) until combined. Add extra salt and pepper to taste.
- Transfer vegetables to a serving platter or bowl, and drizzle with the prepared dressing. Serve immediately.

Vietnamese Style Grilled Lemongrass Pork

Ingredients
- 800g Pork Shoulder, sliced to about ½ inch thick pieces
- 6 cloves garlic
- 2 pcs shallots, roughly chopped
- 2 stalk lemongrass (white part only)
- 1 tbsp dark soy sauce
- ¼ cup fish sauce
- 3 tbsp oil
- freshly ground black pepper
- ½ cup honey

Directions
- Place garlic, shallots, lemongrass, dark soy sauce, fish sauce, oil and freshly ground black pepper in a food processor, process until it becomes a paste.
- Place pork in a deep bowl and pour marinade mix, coat pork pieces evenly then cover your bowl. Marinate for 24 hours.
- Remove 2 hours from fridge before cooking, then cook over charcoal barbecue for best results. On medium high heat grill each side for 3-4 minutes.
- Dip each pork pieces in honey and grill for 2 more minutes on side.

- Serve while hot.

Grilled Corn

Ingredients
- 5 pieces of corn on the cob, husks removed
- 2 tbsp. olive oil
- Salt and black pepper to taste
- 1/4 cup mayonnaise
- 1/2 cup parmesan cheese, finely grated
- 2 tbsp. garlic powder
- 3 tbsp. paprika
- 1 tbsp. cayenne pepper
- 5 lime wedges

Directions
- Preheat your barbecue on medium heat. In the meantime, coat corn cobs with olive oil and evenly sprinkle salt and pepper for taste.
- Once preheated, place the corn on the grill and cook for 12-15 minutes turning every 5 minutes or so. When finished, the corn should be lightly browned or blackened just enough for the kernels to be cooked.

- Cover each piece in the mayonnaise (as you would butter with regular corn on the cob), then sprinkle parmesan cheese, garlic powder, paprika and cayenne pepper.
- Serve with lime wedges and squeeze the juice over the corn before eating for an extra flavour blast.

Rosemary Shrimp Skewers with Arugula-White Bean Salad

Ingredients
- 3 tablespoons plus 1 teaspoon extra virgin olive oil
- 3 tablespoons plus 2 teaspoons fresh lemon juice
- 3 garlic cloves, smashed
- 2 teaspoons minced fresh rosemary
- 3/4 teaspoon salt
- 1/4 teaspoon plus 1/8 teaspoon black pepper
- 1 1/2 pounds extra-large shrimp, shelled and cleaned, tails on
- Nonstick cooking spray
- 1 small garlic clove, minced
- Pinch sugar
- 1 5-ounce package baby arugula
- 1 15-ounce can cannellini beans, rinsed and drained
- 1/2 small red onion, thinly sliced

Directions
- Combine 2 tablespoons of the olive oil, 1 tablespoon of the lemon

juice, the smashed garlic cloves, the rosemary, 1/2 teaspoon of the salt,
and 1/4 teaspoon of the black pepper in a medium bowl.
- Add the shrimp; toss well. Cover and refrigerate 15 minutes.
- Heat a grill to medium-high. Thread shrimp on skewers and discard marinade. Lightly mist grill with cooking spray.
- Grill shrimp until just cooked through, about 2 minutes per side.
Combine the minced garlic, sugar, and remaining olive oil, lemon juice, salt, and black pepper in a large bowl.
- Add the arugula, beans, and onion; toss to combine. Mound the salad on one side of a large platter and arrange the
shrimp skewers alongside.

Pork & Veggie Kebabs

Ingredients
- 4 tablespoons olive oil
- 2 garlic cloves, chopped
- Zest and juice of 1 lemon
- 2 tablespoons chopped flat-leaf parsley
- 1 tablespoon chopped fresh rosemary
- 1 teaspoon chopped fresh thyme
- 1 teaspoon sugar
- 1/2 teaspoon salt, plus more for serving
- 1/4 teaspoon black pepper
- 1 1/4 pounds boneless pork chops (3/4 to 1 inch thick), cut into 1-inch pieces
- 2 medium zucchini, cut into 1/2-inch slices
- 2 medium summer squash, cut into 1/2-inch slices
- 12 cherry tomatoes

Directions
- For marinade, whisk together oil, garlic, and lemon zest and juice in a small bowl. Stir in parsley, rosemary, thyme, sugar, 1/2 teaspoon salt, and the pepper.

- Place pork in a large resealable bag and spoon in 4 tablespoons of the marinade. Place zucchini, squash, and tomatoes in another large resealable bag; cover with the rest of the marinade. Seal both bags and shake to coat. Refrigerate for 1 hour, turning after 30 minutes.
- Heat a gas grill to medium-high or prepare a charcoal grill with medium-hot coals.
- Thread metal skewers separately with pork and vegetables.
- Grill vegetables about 5 minutes per side and pork about 3 minutes per side, or until internal temperature reads 155 degrees F. on an instant-read thermometer.
- To serve, season with salt to taste.

Grilled Italian Flank Steak Pinwheels

Ingredients

Marinade Ingredients:
- ¼ cup extra virgin olive oil
- ¼ red wine vinegar
- 1 tsp garlic, minced
- 2 Tbsp parsley, chopped
- ¼ tsp black pepper

Pinwheel Ingredients:
- 1½ lb beef flank steak, fat trimmed
- ½ tsp salt
- ½ tsp black pepper
- 2 tsp garlic powder
- 5 The Laughing Cow® Light Garlic and Herb Cheese Wedges
- 2 Tbsp Italian seasoning
- 1½ cups baby spinach, chopped
- ½ cup sundried tomatoes, diced

Other:
- 6 — 12-inch strips of Baker's twine
- 8 wooden skewers, soaked in water for 20 minutes
- PAM grill spray

Instructions
- In a large sealable plastic bag, add marinade ingredients and flank steak. Seal bag and give it a few good shakes to spread the marinade around. Refrigerate for at least one hour.
- Preheat grill to medium-high heat. Remove meat from plastic bag, place between two sheets of wax or parchment paper and use a meal mallet or rolling pin to flatten meat to ¼-inch thick.

- Sprinkle salt, pepper and garlic powder on both sides of meat. Evenly spread Laughing Cow® cheese wedge on one side of the meat, leaving 1-inch of meat around the edges. Next sprinkle with Italian seasoning, add baby spinach and top with sundried tomatoes.
- Start at one edge and roll up tightly. Stuff any ingredients that fall out, back in. Tie Baker's twine tightly around meat, roll in 1 inch intervals. Secure meat with wooden skewers right next to each strip of twine. Slice the roll between the skewers using a sharp butcher's knife to create 6 equally-sized pinwheels + 2 messy end pieces. Grill the end pieces separately.
- Lightly coat the roll with nonstick grill spray. Place steak pinwheels on heated grill. Grill covered, 4-5 minutes on each side or until desired doneness. Let rest for 5 minutes, remove wood skewers, twine and enjoy!

Grilled Rainbow Carrots with basil vinaigrette

Ingredients
- 2 bunches rainbow carrots
- 1 tablespoon safflower oil
- 3 Tablespoons apple cider vinegar
- ¼ cup basil leaves
- ¼ cup extra-virgin olive oil
- salt and pepper to taste

Directions
- Preheat grill over medium-high heat.
- Trim carrot tops and slice carrots in half lengthwise (this decreases cooking time).
- Toss carrots with oil (or oil grill if needed) and grill for 4-5 minutes, until the carrots develop sear marks and are beginning to soften. Flip, cover, and grill for another 4-5 minutes.
- Carrots should be softened, but still retain their crunch.
- Meanwhile blend the vinegar, basil, and olive oil to create the vinaigrette. Serve drizzled over the carrots or on the side for dipping. Add salt and pepper to taste if desired.

- Serve warm or at room temperature. Carrots can also be sliced into smaller pieces before serving.

Asian Grilled and Glazed Chicken Skewers

Ingredients
- 3 tablespoons plus 2 tablespoons Ah-So sauce
- 2 tablespoons soy sauce
- 3 tablespoons brown sugar
- 2 teaspoons ground ginger
- 2 garlic cloves, minced
- 1 pound chicken breast, cut length-wise into 1 ½-inch-wide strips
- wooden skewers, soaked in water for 20 minutes before using
- 2 tablespoons maple syrup

Directions
- In a small bowl, whisk 3 tablespoons of the Ah-So sauce, soy sauce, brown sugar, ginger, garlic, and 1 tablespoon water.
- Put the chicken strips in a gallon-sized re-sealable plastic bag. Pour the marinade over the chicken, squeeze as much air out of the bag as possible, and seal it. Turn the bag in your hands a few times to coat all of the chicken strips in marinade. Refrigerate for at least 1 hour and up to 24 hours before grilling.

- Make the glaze by whisking the remaining 2 tablespoons of Ah-So sauce and the maple syrup in a small bowl. Set aside.
- Preheat your gas grill to medium-high heat. Remove the chicken strips from the marinade, discarding the remaining sauce, and carefully thread one strip of chicken onto a wooden skewer, leaving enough of the wood exposed on one end to allow for you to hold the skewer like a popsicle. Set the prepared strip on a large, rimmed baking sheet while you repeat the threading process with the rest of the chicken.
- Grill the skewers for 4 to 5 minutes per side, until the chicken is opaque and cooked through. Once all the skewers are cooked, use a pastry brush to lightly coat each chicken skewer with the Ah-So-Maple glaze. Serve immediately.

Grilled Pineapple Chicken Sandwich

Ingredients
- 4 — 4 oz boneless, skinless chicken breasts
- 1½ cups of reduced-sodium teriyaki marinade
- 3 Tbsp chili mayonnaise
- 4 pineapple rings, fresh or canned in it's own juice
- 4 whole grain sandwich thins

Chili Mayonnaise
- ½ cup light mayo (nutrition calculated with 1/4 cup)
- 2 tsp lime juice
- 3 tsp Thai chili sauce

Optional Toppings
- lettuce
- tomato

Directions
- Place chicken breasts in a shallow baking pan or dish. You can even place chicken in a Ziploc® storage bag.
- Generously cover the chicken with the teriyaki marinade with 1 cup of marinade.
- Place chicken in refrigerator for at least 3 hours or even overnight for additional flavor.
- Using non-stick cooking spray, lightly coat an indoor or outdoor grill.

- Cook chicken on grill, turning to cook evenly on both sides.
- Use remaining ½ cup of marinade on chicken while grilling, but reserve ¼ cup to use with pineapples.
- After chicken has cooked, remove chicken and set aside.
- Add pineapple rings to grill and add ¼ cup of marinade to pineapple rings while cooking. Cook for 2-3 minutes until pineapple is heated through.
- Add sandwich thins to grill and grill both sides until golden brown.
- To assemble sandwiches stack chicken breast, pineapple rings and Chili Mayonnaise to buns and serve immediately.

Chili Mayonnaise
- Whisk all ingredients together in a small bowl. Refrigerate until serving.

Lemon Parmesan Foil-Pack Broccoli

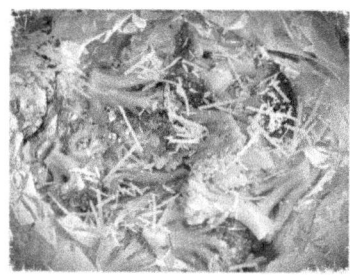

Ingredients
- 1 bag (12 oz) Green Giant™ Steamers™ Select™ frozen broccoli florets
- 1 tablespoon lemon juice
- 1 tablespoon olive oil
- ½ teaspoon salt
- ¼ teaspoon pepper
- 3 tablespoons shredded Parmesan cheese

Directions
- Heat gas or charcoal grill to medium-high heat. Tear off 2 (12-inch) lengths Reynolds Wrap® Heavy Duty Foil to make foil packets. Place half the broccoli in center of each piece of foil. Drizzle with lemon juice, olive oil and salt and pepper.
- Bring up 2 sides of foil so edges meet. Seal edges, making tight 1/2-inch fold; fold again, allowing space on sides for heat circulation and expansion. Fold other sides to seal.
- Place foil packets on grill over indirect heat. Cover grill; cook 15 to 25 minutes or until broccoli is heated through. Carefully open foil packs, and sprinkle broccoli with Parmesan cheese. Serve immediately.

Grilled Avocado with Melted Cheese & Hot Sauce

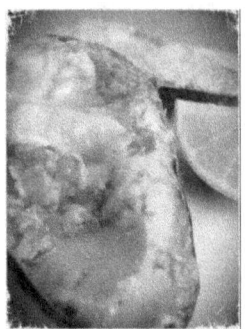

Ingredients
1 avocado
- 1 tablespoon chipotle sauce (Tabasco or Louisiana)
- 1 tablespoon lime juice
- ¼ cup parmesan cheese
- Salt and pepper

Directions
- Slice the avocado in half and remove the stone. Prick all over with a fork, or cut criss-cross patterns with a knife. This allows the sauce to penetrate the flesh.
- Pour the sauce over each half. Top with lime juice and salt and pepper.
- In the cavity where the stone has been, put a fourth of the cheese on each avocado half. Place under the hot grill for 2 minutes.
- Top with remaining cheese and grill for another 2 minutes until completely melted and avocado warmed through.
- Eat hot with a wedge of lime and chipotle sauce on the side!

Cheddar Bacon BBQ Grilled Potatoes

Ingredients
- 6-8 red potatoes
- ½ sweet yellow onion
- 1 cup bacon bits
- 2 cups shredded cheddar cheese, divided
- ⅓ cup KC Masterpiece® Kansas City Classic barbecue sauce

Directions
- Slice potatoes into ¼ inch thick slices and slice onion into ½ inch slices.
- Spray a foil baking dish with non stick cooking spray.
- Layer potatoes and onions in baking dish. Top with bacon bits, half of the cheese and bbq sauce.
- Cover tightly with a double layer of aluminum foil.
- Grill over medium heat for 30-45 minutes. Be sure to give the potatoes a shake every 5 minutes or so to redistribute them and prevent burning.

Garlic Rubbed Roasted Cabbage Steaks

Ingredients
- 1 (approx 2lb) head of organic green cabbage, cut into 1" thick slices
- 1.5 tablespoons olive oil
- 2 to 3 large garlic cloves, smashed
- kosher salt
- freshly ground black pepper
- spray olive oil OR non-stick cooking spray

Directions
- Preheat oven to 400F and spray a baking sheet with non-stick cooking spray. Pull outer leaf off cabbage (it's usually dirty and nasty looking), cut cabbage from top to bottom (bottom being root) into 1" thick slices.
- Rub both sides of cabbage with smashed garlic.
- Use a pastry brush to evenly spread the olive oil over both sides of the cabbage slices.
- Finally, sprinkle each side with a bit of kosher salt and freshly cracked black pepper.
- Roast on the middle rack for 30 minutes. Carefully flip the cabbage steaks and roast for an additional 30 minutes until edges are brown and crispy. Serve hot and Enjoy!

Grilled Corn Fritters

Ingredients
- ⅓ cup yellow cornmeal
- ¼ cup all-purpose flour
- ½ teaspoon baking powder
- 1 teaspoon kosher salt, or more to taste
- ½ teaspoon ground black pepper Handful of parsley, finely chopped
- ⅓ cup milk 2 cups grilled corn
- Vegetable oil

Directions
- In a large bowl whisk together cornmeal, flour, baking powder, salt, pepper, and parsley. Add milk and mix together with a wooden spoon until thick and thoroughly mixed through. Add the grilled corn and mix well with the flour mixture until all the kernels are well-coated.
- Heat up a skillet over medium high heat and add some vegetable oil to the pan.
- Using a ⅓ cup measuring cup, scoop corn mixture out and place into the skillet, gently pressing the mound down so it's flattened. Cook for 5 minutes on one side, or until it's browned, flip, and cook another 5 minutes, or until it's browned. Remove and repeat for all the other corn fritters.
- Serve immediately.

Eggs On the Grill

Ingredients
12 eggs

Directions
- Preheat an outdoor grill for medium high heat and lightly oil grate.
- Coat all holes of a muffin pan with cooking spray and crack an egg into each hole.
- Place on grill and grill over medium high heat for 2 minutes, or to desired doneness.

Grilled Seafood Packs with Lemon-Chive Butter

Ingredients

Seafood Packets
- 32 shell clams (littlenecks or cherrystones)
- 32 uncooked medium shrimp in shells (about 1 1/4 lb), thawed if frozen
- 32 sea scallops (about 2 1/2 lb)
- 4 ears fresh sweet corn, husks removed, cleaned, cut into fourths
- 32 large cherry tomatoes

Lemon-Chive Butter
- 1/3 cup butter or margarine, melted
- 2 teaspoons grated lemon peel
- 2 teaspoons chopped fresh or 1/2 teaspoon freeze-dried chives
- Fresh chive stems or chopped fresh chives, if desired

Directions
- Heat gas or charcoal grill. Cut 8 (18x12-inch) sheets of heavy-duty foil; spray with cooking spray.
- Place 4 clams, shrimp and scallops in center of each sheet; top each with 2 pieces of corn and 4 tomatoes. In small bowl,

- mix butter ingredients. Drizzle about 2 teaspoons butter over seafood and vegetables in each packet.
- Bring up 2 sides of foil so edges meet. Seal edges, making tight 1/2-inch fold; fold again, allowing space for heat circulation and expansion. Fold other sides to seal.
- Place packets on grill over medium heat. Cover grill; cook 15 to 20 minutes, rotating packets 1/2 turn after 10 minutes, or until clam shells have opened, shrimp are pink, and scallops are white and opaque. (Cooking time may vary depending on ingredients selected) Discard any clams that don't open.
- To serve, cut large X across top of each packet; carefully fold back foil to allow steam to escape. Top with chives.

Grill Broiled Sirloin Steak

Ingredients
- beef sirloin steak, cut
- 1-inch thick
- salt
- pepper

Directions
- Place steak on grill over ash-covered coals so the surface of steak is 2 to 3 inches from the heat.
- Broil at moderate temperature. When one side is browned, turn, season and finish cooking on the second side.
- Turn and season. A steak cut 1 inch thick requires 18 to 20 minutes for rare and 20 to 25 minutes for medium.

Grill Chicken With Havana Sauce

Ingredients
- 28 oz plum tomatoes, drained and
- 1/3 c olive oil
- 1/4 c white wine
- 1 T white vinegar
- 3green onions, chopped
- 4 c garlic, minced
- 1/2 t salt
- 1/2 t pepper
- 2 t cilantro, minced
- 8chicken, breasts , skin re
    - pepper, Ground

Directions

- In large bowl combine all the ingredients for the sauce. Mix well, cover and refrigerate over night.
- Heat an outside grill and let the sauce come to room temp. Sprinkle the chicken with lime juice and with salt and pepper, as you like.
- Place on grill and cook for about 6 min per side or until brown. Brush the sauce on the chicken throughout the grilling and top each with more sauce when serving.

Grill Poached Salmon

Ingredients
- 2 lb salmon fillets -- (or steaks)
- 2 T butter
- t salt
- 6 sl lemon -- (thin)
- 1/2 c white wine
- few grains pepper

Directions
- Cut salmon into serving-size pieces. Place each piece on a square of heavy duty aluminum foil. Double thickness of foil may be used.
- Sprinkle salmon with salt and pepper, top with butter, a slice of lemon and drizzle with wine.
- Close package securely and cook on the grill for 20-30 minutes or until fish flakes easily when tested with a fork.

Grilled 'napalm' Shrimp

Ingredients
- 2 lb shrimp 20-26 count
- large habanero chili stem removed chopped
- 1/2 stick butter
- 1 1/2 T onion --,Chopped
- 1 T cayenne
- t Worcestershire sauce
- 1 t lemon juice
- 1/2 t pepper

- 1/2 t paprika
- 1/2 t cumin seed --,Ground
- 1 T brown sugar
- bamboo skewers

Directions

- First, peel and de-vein shrimp. Wash, drain and place on skewers 5- 6 per skewers.
- Sauté onions and garlic in butter, remove from heat and place in blender.
- Add cayenne, Worcestershire sauce, lemon juice pepper, cumin, brown sugar and the habaneros with seeds.
- Blend till smooth. Brush onto the shrimp skewers and marinate for 30-60 min. in fridge.
- Start grill and cook till opaque and slightly crispy dust with paprika and serve.

Grilled Acorn Squash~ Mushroom & Asparagus

Ingredients
- 4acorn squash -- and, Halved cleaned
- salt and pepper --,To Taste
- 4sprigs rosemary
- 4 T onions --,Minced
- 4 T celery --,Minced
- 4 T carrots --,Minced
- 4 T olive oil
- c vegetable stock
- lb quinoa -- washed
- lb fresh mushrooms -- wild
- lb asparagus -- pencil
- preferred

Directions
- Rub acorn squash with salt, pepper, oil and rosemary vigorously, inside. Grill face down for 8 minutes. Turn over, put rosemary inside and cook, covered for 20minutes.
- In a pot, place onions, celery, carrots and 1 tablespoon olive oil and cook. Add stock and quinoa and bring to a boil. Cover tightly and simmer for 10 minutes. Uncover squash, place quinoa mixture inside squash and cover. Cook for an additional 10 minutes.
- Lightly toss mushrooms and asparagus with olive oil, salt and pepper.
- Grill for 3 minutes on each side. Serve squash with quinoa inside and have mushrooms and asparagus flowing around.

Grilled Angel Food Cake With Nectarines & Blu

Ingredients
- 6 ripe nectarines
- 3 T powdered sugar
- zest of 1 lemon, Grated
- juice of 1/2 a lemon
- 6 sl angel food cake
- pt fresh blueberries

Directions
- Prepare grill & cover to build an intense heat. Remove nectarine pits & slice each one into 6 slices.
- Combine sugar, zest, lemon juice in a small bowl. Place 6 nectarine slices on a skewer & place on grill.
- Cook 5 minutes, turn & baste with glaze. Cook & baste for another 7 minutes.

When fruit is just about done, toast cake slices on a cooler part of the grill, turning once. Serve toasted cake with grilled nectarines & handfuls of blueberries.

Grilled Apple-Nut Stuffed Pork Chops

Ingredients
APPLE NUT STUFFING
- c soft bread crumbs
- 1/2 c apple, chopped
- T pecans, chopped
- 1/4 t nutmeg
- 1/4 t salt

PORK CHOPS
- 4 pork chops, 1 thick
- 1/4 c margarine (or butter), melt
- 1/4 c orange juice
- 1/4 t nutmeg

Directions
- Prepare apple-nut stuffing by mixing all ingredients. Cut a deep pocket in each pork chop on meatiest side of bone. Press about 1/3 cup stuffing into each pocket.
- Secure with toothpicks. Mix margarine, orange juice and nutmeg.
- Cover and grill pork 4-5" from medium-low coals about 40-45 minutes, brushing occasionally with orange juice mix and turning 3-4 times, until pork is no longer pink in center.
- Remove toothpicks.

Grilled Asian-Spiced Mango & Chicken

Ingredients
- 1/2 c reduced-sodium soy sauce
- 1/4 c olive oil
- T garlic, minced
- T fresh ginger, minced
- T juniper berries, crushed
- T orange peel, Grated
- 4 boneless chicken breasts skinless (about 1-1/2 lb firm, ripe mangoes,(about 2 lb total)
- oranges
- 1 T coriander, Ground
- 1 T Chinese five spice powder
- 1/4 t salt
- 1/4 t pepper
- 1/4 c balsamic vinegar
- 1 T Dijon mustard
- 6 c frisee salad greens,(about 1/2 lb),root ends
- 8 c butter leaves,(about 1 lb)
- 1/2 c raspberries (optional)

Directions
- In a large bowl, combine soy, oil, garlic, ginger, juniper berries, and orange peel. Add chicken; marinate 15 minute, turning often.
- Meanwhile, with a sharp knife, cut skin from mangoes. Cut 2 rounded cheeks from each pit. Trim remaining 1/2-inch of flesh from edge of each mango; mince these trimmings and reserve for mango vinaigrette.
- Cut and discard peel and white membrane from oranges. Slice each orange crosswise into 6 rounds; set aside.

- Combine coriander, five spice, salt, pepper. Lift chicken from marinade; place on a baking sheet (reserve marinade for basting).
- Set mango cheeks on a lightly oiled grill above a solid bed of hot coals in a barbecue with a lid, or use a gas grill on high heat (you can hold your hand at grill level only 2 to 3 seconds); close lid on gas grill. Baste chicken and mango with reserved marinade.
- Using a spatula, turn chicken and mangoes when they start to brown, in about 5 minutes. Baste again; cover barbecue.
- Let chicken and mango cook until no pink remains when chicken is cut in thickest part, about 15 to 20 minutes; turn and baste chicken and mangoes every 5 minutes (depending on mango ripeness, cooking time may be less than for the chicken; remove mangoes when soft and seared).
- Meanwhile, combine minced mango with vinegar and mustard. Mix with frisee and lettuce. Evenly divide among 4 dinner plates.
- Lay mangoes cut side down; slice each into 3/8-inch wide slices, starting 1/2 inch from top down through wide bottom end.
- With a wide spatula, transfer slices to plates atop greens. Gently fan slices apart. Lay chicken and oranges next to mangoes; sprinkle with raspberries.

Grilled Asparagus & Ginger-Lemon Vinaigrette

Ingredients
- lb Young Tender Asparagus
- TB Fresh Ginger -- very finely minced
- 1/3 c Fresh Lemon Juice
- 1/2 c Light Vegetable Oil
- 1/2 TB Toasted Sesame Oil
- teaspoon Sugar
- Salt And Freshly Ground
- Pepper To Taste

Garnish
- TB Lightly Toasted Sesame Seeds

Directions
- Lightly oil asparagus and season with salt and pepper. Grill over hot coals until crisp tender and serve warm or at room temperature with Ginger Lemon Dressing drizzled over.
- Garnish with toasted sesame seeds.

Grilled Asparagus With Lemon Dip

Ingredients
- T olive oil
- lb asparagus, ends broken off
- salt and, Freshly Ground -pepper
- lemon dip
- 1/4 c mayonnaise
    - t lemon rind, Grated
- T lemon juice
- pepper, Freshly Ground

Directions
- Preheat grill to high. Brush oil on asparagus. Place across grill and cook for 2 to 3 minutes per side or until crisp-tender.
- Season with salt and pepper.
- To make lemon dip, combine ingredients. Season to taste. Eat with fingers.

Grilled Balsamic Veal Chops

Ingredients
- shallots
- garlic cloves
- sprigs fresh rosemary
- c balsamic vinegar, divided
- 1/2 c olive oil
- 1/2 t kosher salt
- 1/2 t black pepper
- veal chops,10 oz each
- c balsamic vinegar
- t basil-infused oil
- sprigs fresh thyme (garnish)

Directions
- To be served with Balsamic Ratatouille and Mashed Potatoes w/Mascarpone Cheese & Roasted Garlic

- Roughly chop shallots, garlic and rosemary. Place in a casserole dish large enough to hold the veal chops, along with 2 cups balsamic vinegar and the olive oil, salt, and pepper. Add chops, cover, and marinate in the refrigerator for 6 to 8 hours.
- Remove veal chops from marinade. Place on a hot grill. Cook at medium temperature, turning once, for 9 to 13 minutes, until done to your liking.
- Meanwhile, reduce remaining 1 cup balsamic vinegar by placing it in a small saucepan. Heat over low heat, stirring frequently, until thick and syrupy, about 8 to 10 minutes. (Do not let vinegar boil rapidly or it will burn.) You will get about 4 teaspoons.

- To assemble: On a warm plate, place 1/4 of the ratatouille in the center of each plate. Place 1/4 of the mashed potatoes on top of each serving of ratatouille.
- Drizzle 1 teaspoon basil oil over each serving of potatoes. Lay grilled chops over potatoes and drizzle 1 teaspoon reduced balsamic vinegar over each.
- Garnish with thyme sprigs.

Grilled Bananas

Ingredients
- 12green bananas
- Confectioners sugar

Directions
- Grill unpeeled bananas 4 inches from medium coals, turning once, for 20 minutes or until peel is black and bananas soft.
- Split and sprinkle with sugar. Serve banana in peel, slit and topped with sour cream and toasted coconut.

Grilled Barbeque Chicken Breasts

Ingredients
- 4whole chicken breasts boneless, skinless
- T peanut oil
- salt --,To Taste
- black pepper
    - c barbeque sauce
- watermelon pico de gallo

Directions
- Preheat grill. Make sure grates are clean and lightly rubbed with oil.
- Brush chicken breasts with 2 tablespoons peanut oil and season with salt and pepper.
- Place on grill and cook for 5 minutes, basting with prepared barbeque sauce.
- Turn over, baste with barbeque sauce, and cook for about 5 minutes more or until juices run clear.

Grilled Beef Blade Steaks With Spicy Orange

Ingredients
- large bell pepper -- quartered
- zest of c orange juice
- 1/3 c vegetable oil
- cloves garlic
- tablespoon soy sauce
- teaspoon cider vinegar
- 1/2 teaspoon salt
- teaspoon red pepper flakes
- boneless beef blade steaks pierced all over
- navel oranges

Directions
- In a large shallow pan arrange the blade steaks in one layer and add the bell peppers.
- In a blender, blend the orange zest, juice, oil, garlic, soy sauce, red pepper flakes, vinegar, and the salt until the marinade is smooth, pour over the steaks and the peppers coating them thoroughly and letting the mixture marinate, covered and chilled overnight.

- Grill the steaks and the peppers, discard the marinade, on an oiled rack 5-6 inches over the coals for 8 min. each side for med-rare.
- Transfer the steaks to a platter and let the steaks stand for 5 min.

Grilled Beef Kabobs

Ingredients
- lb stew meat -- cut into 1 inch
- 1/2 c teriyaki sauce
- 1/3 c dry red wine
- T Worcestershire sauce
- 1/2 t garlic salt
- unseasoned meat, Instant tenderizer
- 1/2 small pineapple (or),Canned
- large green pepper -- cut into 1 inch
  - large onion -- cut into 1 inch

Directions
- Place meat in bowl. Mix teriyaki sauce, wine, Worcestershire sauce, and garlic salt.
- Pour over meat. Cover and refrigerate overnight or let stand at room temperature for 2 hours, stirring occasionally.
- Drain meat, reserving marinade. Sprinkle meat with tenderizer according to package directions.
- Prepare pineapple, cut into wedges. On four skewers thread meat alternately with green pepper, pineapple, and onion.
- Grill over hot coals 8 minutes, baste with marinade. Turn, grill 7 minutes more. (Or broil 4-5 inches from heat for 8

minutes, turn, baste, then grill 7 minutes more). Brush once more.

Grilled Beef Tenderloin With Red Wine & Pis

Ingredients
- c beef (or veal stock)
- c dry red wine – preferably pinot noir
- 1/2 c roasted garlic cloves
- 1/2 c shallots, Chopped
- 1/2 c fresh parsley, Chopped
- ds each salt and pepper
- 1/4 c toasted pistachios, chopped
- 1/4 c sunflower seeds -,Toasted chopped
- lb beef tenderloin - cut in 8oz. steaks
  - T olive oil (or corn oil)

GARNISH
- 4fresh parsley sprigs

Directions
- Preheat grill or broiler.
- To make Red Wine Sauce: In a large saucepan, combine the stock, red wine, 3 tablespoons of the roasted garlic, shallots and 1/4 cup of chopped parsley.
- Bring to a simmer over medium heat; cook until reduced to coat the back of a spoon, about 20 minutes.
- Transfer to a blender; puree until smooth. Strain through a fine sieve into another saucepan, then adjust the salt and pepper. Stir in the remaining parsley; reduce heat to low.
- In a small bowl, combine the remaining garlic, pistachios, sunflower seeds and 2 tablespoons of the Red Wine Sauce. Mix well. Rub the surface of the steaks with the oil.

- Grill steaks until well-seared on the surface, about 5 minutes. Turn over and cook until you reach desired doneness, about 4 minutes for medium-rare, depending on the thickness.
- Brush tops of steaks with a small amount of Red Wine Sauce, then press the steaks, top side down, into the pistachio mixture, coating the surface well. Position the steaks on serving plates, spoon the remaining sauce around them, garnish with parsley sprigs and serve.

Grilled Blue Cheese Slices

Ingredients

- 1/4 c (1/2 stick) margarine or -butter softened
- 1/4 c blue cheese, Crumbled
  - T parmesan cheese, Grated
- 1/2 loaf (1 lb.) French bread

Directions

- Mix margarine and cheeses. Cut bread horizontally in half. Spread one cut side with cheese mixture. Top with remaining bread half.
- Wrap in heavy-duty aluminum foil. Grill bread 5 to 6 inches from medium coals about 6 minutes, turning once, until hot.
- Slices.

- Grilled Pepper Cheese Slices: Omit Parmesan cheese. Substitute ½ cup shredded pepper Jack cheese for the blue cheese. Mix margarine and cheese.
- Grilled Herb-Lemon Cheese Slices: Omit blue cheese and Parmesan cheese. Mix margarine, 2 tsp. chopped fresh herbs or 1/2 tsp. dried herbs, 1 tsp. lemon juice and dash of salt.

Grilled Bluefish Wrapped In Mammoth Basil Leaf

Ingredients
- 10 mature mammoth basil leaves- (fresh)
- 1/2 lb bluefish
- 4 T pesto

Directions
- Heat outdoor grill. Soak the Mammoth basil leaves in water. Slice the bluefish into strips 2 inches wide, making 8 slices.
- Spread pesto on each slice of fish. Wrap each slice in a Mammoth basil leaf, securing with a toothpick or wooden skewer.
- Place the wrapped fish on the hot grill over glowing coals, 6 inches from the heat. Cover the grill and cook for 5 minutes on each side.

www.ingramcontent.com/pod-product-compliance
Lightning Source LLC
Chambersburg PA
CBHW071438070526
44578CB00001B/129